You Can ADOPT *Without* DEBT

Creative Ways to Cover the Cost of Adoption

JULIE GUMM

Abingdon Press

Nashville

YOU CAN ADOPT WITHOUT DEBT
Creative Ways to Cover the Cost of Adoption

Copyright 2014 © by Julie Gumm

Library of Congress Cataloging-in-Publication Data

Gumm, Julie.
    You can adopt without debt : creative ways to cover the cost of adoption / Julie Gumm
    pages cm
    ISBN 978-1-4267-9300-4 (alk. paper)
    1. Adoption—Religious aspects—Christianity.   2. Adoption—United States.
3. Adoption agencies—Fees.   4. Fund raising.   I. Title.
    HV875.26.G86 2014
    362.7340973—dc23

                                                                     2014019119

Unless otherwise indicated, all Scripture quotations are taken from the *Holy Bible*, New Living Translation, copyright © 1996, 2004, 2007. Used by permission of Tyndale House Publishers, Inc., Carol Stream, Illinois 60188. All rights reserved.

Scripture quotations marked (NIV) are taken from the Holy Bible, New International Version®, NIV®. Copyright © 1973, 1978, 1984, 2011 by Biblica, Inc.™ Used by permission of Zondervan. All rights reserved worldwide. www.zondervan.com. The "NIV" and "New International Version" are trademarks registered in the United States Patent and Trademark Office by Biblica, Inc.™

14 15 16 17 18 19 20 21 22 23—10 9 8 7 6 5 4 3 2 1
MANUFACTURED IN THE UNITED STATES OF AMERICA

3 0646 00221 9206

For Wendemagegn and Beza,
Who opened their hearts and let me be their Mom

For Noah and Natalie,
Who embraced their new brother and sister

For Mark,
Who listened to God—and your crazy wife

CONTENTS

ACKNOWLEDGMENTS

I am so grateful to all the families that shared their struggles, their successes, and their stories within the pages of this book. Many of you have become friends through this process, and I consider it a joy to watch your families grow, even if only through Facebook photos.

To Mark, my husband of twenty-one years, I love you! The twenty-year-old girl who stood beside you in that church had *no* idea of the wild ride God would take us on but I wouldn't trade it for anything. You are my rock, my partner in parenting and ministry, and I couldn't do life without you. Thank you for all the mornings you let me sleep in until 11:00 after a late night of writing, for all the loads of laundry you did, and for all the nights you put up with leftovers because I had no energy left to cook. I look forward to what God has for us with amazement, excitement, and anticipation.

Luke, Noah, Beza, and Natalie—thanks for putting up with me during this crazy process. We will now return to our normally scheduled life.

I am grateful for all the support and excitement shown by countless friends, particularly my amazing cheerleading squad—Jen, Stacey, and Kristen. Your anticipation and joy helped fuel me. Your gentle (and not-so-gentle) nudges kept me going even when doubts and fear interrupted me.

Mom and Dad, thank you for always believing I was capable of great things. I've come a long way from the little girl who used to write notes and stuff them in Dad's sock drawer. I could not have done it without your love and support.

To the rest of my immediate family—Brad, Suzanne, Phil, Tricia, Billy, Cathy, Matt, Hollie, Jenny, and Rob—God gave me the greatest gift when He put you in my life. Each of you fills a special role and has played a vital part in our adoption journey. Thank you for your love and support.

Gary Warner, my John Brown University journalism professor, taught me more than just the mechanics of writing and editing. He taught me to never settle for hurried and uninspired writing—but to do this thing that I love with excellence. I am forever grateful.

I am amazed at the God-orchestrated circumstances that brought me to my agent, Blythe Daniel. Many writers search for years for an agent who believes in their work but God was clearly in control. Thank you, Blythe, for your encouragement and for finding the perfect home for my book.

I also have to thank Becky Wilmoth for sharing her expertise and answering my questions about the adoption tax credit. She's the expert I point everyone to and a great resource. Cheri Walrod of Resources 4 Adoption, a.k.a. "the Grant Guru," shares my same heart for helping families, and I appreciate the valuable resource that she is.

Thank you to all the staff at Abingdon Press who believe in this book and worked so hard to get it into the hands of adoptive families. You are now part of the ripple effect and helping children find forever families!

At the heart of this book is a simple message that God continues to whisper in our ears, "Follow me, I will provide." Mark and I have experienced that truth countless times in our marriage, but never as profoundly as during our adoption process. I am amazed and humbled that He would use me to share that message with others. A line in one of my favorite songs echoes in my heart "Forever, You are the God of my story. Write every line for Your glory." That is my simple prayer.

INTRODUCTION

People often ask, "When did you first start to think about adopting?" Truth is I can't pinpoint an exact time. The idea of adoption kind of crept in and out of our lives over many years.

As a seventeen-year-old, I spent two years working for an adoption attorney who handled both private adoptions and court-appointed legal matters for children in the state foster care system. Typing legal briefs and court papers opened my eyes to both the incredible heartache in some of the children's lives, as well as the joy of the chosen adoptive parents. I even briefly entertained the idea of going into family law, but once in college I pursued my love of writing instead.

When I graduated high school I ended up in northwest Arkansas at a private Christian university, John Brown University. Mark, who I had been dating for two years, was already there. After two more years of dating, we married in the summer of 1993.

Together, God took us on a long and winding road that eventually led to adoption. But not before we made a lot of financial mistakes and eventually learned to be good stewards of the money God had entrusted to us. In truth, our financial journey led to our adoption journey.

We finished college and began life in the Army with Mark serving four years in return for his ROTC scholarship. Life felt full of possibilities and, to be honest, full of entitlements. We had spent two years as poor, married college students and were ready for the double-income, no-kids period.

Before we knew it we had $8,000 in credit card debt piled on top of our student loans and car payments. We spent the next four years

1

in a vicious cycle of budgeting, paying down our debt, failing, and being right back in the same place.

In the midst of our debt cycle we decided to start a family. After a year of trying and no pregnancy, I wondered if perhaps God intended my early experience with the adoption world to prepare me for an adoption journey of our own. I wasn't necessarily against it, but I desperately wanted to get pregnant.

Turns out all I needed was a little more patience. Six months later I became pregnant with our son, Noah, who was born in October of 1999. Mark, now out of the Army, had just begun a job that involved a forty-five-minute commute each way. During his drive home one day he discovered *The Dave Ramsey Show*—a nationally syndicated radio show on personal finance.

Now, remember that I'd been cooped up in the house all day with a new crying baby who was still learning to breastfeed. I may or may not have managed a shower. I can guarantee I was sleep deprived and, of course, those pesky post-pregnancy hormones were *all* over the place.

Mark would stroll in the door, kiss me and the baby hello, and launch into what he'd learned from Dave Ramsey that day. "Dave Ramsey says we should pay cash for everything. Dave Ramsey says we should use the envelope system. Dave Ramsey says we should pay off the smallest debt first. Dave Ramsey says..." Blah, blah, blah. I was quite tempted to throw the balled up, wet diaper sitting next to me toward his head.

Nine months later we were living in Phoenix, and our financial system was not working any better. We knew we were making perfectly good money, but we had no idea where it was all going. So when a Dave Ramsey Financial Peace Live seminar (now called "Dave Ramsey Live") came to town, I agreed to give up my Saturday and go. By the end of the five-hour seminar I was a believer.

Mark and I were both energized and motivated to get control of our finances. We were still young—twenty-eight and twenty-seven, respectively—and excited about what a debt-free future would mean.

While it may seem completely unrelated to adoption, this journey to becoming debt-free would be a major catalyst in our decision.

While I didn't dream of palatial mansions and exotic cars, I will admit the allure of being debt-free involved retiring at age fifty, traveling the world, and renting a house on the beach every summer.

So we began to work the "Seven Baby Steps" in Dave Ramsey's plan. We got $1,000 into a savings account within a couple months. Next we tackled all our debt (except for the house). At the time we had two car payments, student loans, and credit card debt totaling about $30,000.

We adjusted our spending habits. We created a budget and made sure we knew where every dollar was going. It's not that we lived on beans and rice, but eating out became a treat, not a weekly occurrence. We downgraded the satellite package, and I cut back on the frequency of my clothes shopping. We sold our SUV and were given my grandmother's car when she passed away.

Within two years we had paid off all our debts and had a nice $10,000 emergency fund in place. It was the most amazing feeling! With our house on a fifteen-year mortgage, we envisioned being debt-free at ages forty-three and forty-two.

With no debt and our savings in place we now had over $1,000 in "discretionary" money every month. What would we do with it? We could adjust our lifestyle up, invest it, or give it generously.

Yes, we did make some adjustments to our budget: added the vacation savings back in, upped the eating-out budget, and increased our personal fun money. But other than a few small things, we'd really grown quite content with our simplified lifestyle.

We'd faithfully given to our church for years. But now we could support friends who were missionaries, sponsor children across the world, and help local families in need of extra help at Christmas. Suddenly using our money to help others became way more fun than spending it on ourselves.

I'm not going to lie; I like a shopping trip as much as the next girl. But as we loosened our hold on our money, we could see God's direct blessings over and over again. One major blessing was that when our daughter, Natalie, was born in 2002 I was able to leave my job and become a stay-at-home mom. Three years earlier I never would have imagined that.

Within the next year, overwhelmed with two kids (and what doctors would later diagnose as clinical depression) I declared myself D-O-N-E! I had a boy and a girl, and I was good. Our family was complete. We were so sure that we took steps to make it permanent. Snip, snip.

Two years later, in 2004, the housing market went nuts. It went a little crazy everywhere, but it went *really* crazy in Phoenix. Houses listed on the market for double their original purchase price and buyers snapped them up in days, sometimes hours.

Mark started crunching numbers and researching—something he loves. Me? I cringed at the thought of moving again. (Three moves in five years wears on a girl, you know?)

But Mark discovered that by downsizing and moving thirteen miles west, we could fast-forward our financial freedom. The math showed us we could sell our current house, put the profit down on a new house, and shrink our mortgage to $65,000. If we really buckled down and attacked that mortgage, we could pay it off in three years.

Suddenly, debt-free at forty-three and forty-two became debt-free at thirty-five and thirty-four.

It was the best financial decision we *ever* made.

With promotions and raises over the years, our budget definitely had some extra room in it and we went back into "gazelle" mode to pay off the house. The light at the end of the tunnel was bright and we were running full-speed!

During this time, my husband worked on staff with our church, among other things, overseeing the benevolence funds and developing an interest in missions and helping people in need.

I continued, as I had for years, to find myself moved by news stories of kids in foster care, kids rescued from abusive situations, and stories of adoption.

I think I even mentioned to Mark that *maybe* we should consider doing short-term emergency foster care. But I was still scared of something more permanent. I envisioned having children for a few days until social services found them permanent foster homes.

But life continued and no big changes were made.

In 2006, Mark met a pastor from Zambia and our church started looking into partnering with him to build an orphanage. When our pastor asked in passing, "Can you adopt from Zambia?" I started doing some research online. From there, I was pretty much a goner—adoption had taken root in my heart. I spent hours researching international adoption and reading dozens of adoption blogs.

One day Mark was reading his Bible in James and he stopped when he read James 1:27: "Religion that God our Father accepts as pure and faultless is this: to look after orphans and widows in their distress and to keep oneself from being polluted by the world" (NIV).

"Do I even know one single orphan?" Mark thought to himself. When he realized he didn't, his heart broke. If caring for widows and orphans in their distress is so close to God's heart, how could we have been so ignorant of His command?

Mark processed all these thoughts internally while I was going through my own journey. Neither of us voiced what God was speaking to us individually.

In May 2007, our best friends, Dustin and Jen Sloniger, announced they had decided to adopt. My ears perked up. I think I even said, "I've thought about doing that."

Over the next several months, I researched international adoption, peppered Jen with questions, and percolated on the idea. Yet Mark and I still hadn't discussed it together. I think I was still figuring out if I really wanted to bring this up—I was still afraid of going down the adoption path. Did I really want to add to our brood? To be honest, some days I thought to myself, "I can barely handle the two kids I have. What makes me think I could take on another?"

In early October 2007, Mark attended the Catalyst Conference with several church staff members. During Dave Ramsey's keynote he shared a video interview with a couple that wanted to adopt. Determined to pay off their debt first, the family had a chance encounter with another couple who offered to pay off their debt so they could start the adoption process. I wasn't there, but I'm pretty sure the video made Mark cry. He left telling a friend, "I want to be that guy."

He sent me a link to the video, and I cried as I watched it too. But I wasn't sure if Mark's reaction meant he wanted to be the guy adopting or the guy paying off the adoptive family's debt. Either way, it was my first clue that God was speaking to my husband about orphans.

A few weeks later, Mark and I were eating lunch at Chipotle, sitting outside enjoying the beautiful Phoenix fall weather. Halfway through the meal, I blurted out, "So what do you think about adopting?"

I honestly expected Mark to fall off the chair or, at the very least, tell me I was nuts. When he didn't, we started talking about what God had whispered to both of us separately.

We discussed what adoption might look like. With Natalie starting kindergarten the next fall, we didn't think we wanted to adopt young kids. We felt like we were done with that part of our lives. Maybe a child somewhere between Noah and Natalie in age? We knew older children are harder to place. For that matter, sibling sets were even harder to place. If we would consider adopting one, why not two?

We mentioned the idea to the kids—that it was something we were considering. I knew Natalie would be overjoyed. She's a social butterfly, and her theory is "the more the merrier." I wasn't sure about Noah, but he was all for it as long as there was at least one boy.

A few weeks later, Mark and I left for a seven-day cruise on the Mexican Riviera—just the two of us celebrating that we had made the *final* house payment that month. We were debt-free!

In my suitcase, I had packed brochures from a dozen different adoption agencies and a stack of printed adoption research. We spent some of that week poring over them, looking at the timelines, the costs, the requirements, and praying for wisdom. By the end of the trip we had decided that yes, we were going to adopt.

We weren't sure where we would adopt from. But in the end, God led us right to our children.

During my requests for information from agencies, I connected with a nonprofit organization working with widows and orphans in Ethiopia. The DVD came, and late one night in early December I popped it into my computer and briefly scanned the disc menu. By that point, we had decided we wanted a sibling group between the ages of five and eight (our kid's ages at the time). We intended to keep Noah as the oldest child, which we thought would be important to him. We were open to two boys, or a boy and a girl.

I watched the clips of two sibling sets that fell within that five-to-eight range.

I clicked on the first one. Both of their parents had died, and they were living with their grandmother, who was sick and concerned about who would care for her grandchildren when she died. As the camera panned to the grandmother, my tears started to flow. I couldn't imagine the pain she was feeling—the personal sacrifice she was making for these children.

The interviewer asked them questions about their favorite foods, what they liked to do in their free time, what grade they were in at school, and so on. The girl was particularly shy and her older brother prompted her several times by nudging her. At the end, the worker asked if they knew any songs. In English, they sang a "Good Morning" song, complete with motions. It was adorable. Their names were Wendemagegn and Beza. He was eight, she was five.

The second sibling group was an eight-year-old boy and seven-year-old girl who were living in an orphanage. They had huge, genuine smiles on their faces and were giggling. They did the same thing, answering questions, singing their ABCs, and so on. Their singing voices were beautiful.

I made Mark come watch the two video clips. When we finished, he didn't say much, and I didn't really know what he was thinking as we headed upstairs to bed.

I went to bed that night, praying that God would watch over the two sibling groups and find them families, even if it wasn't us. I asked God to show us if He wanted us to adopt one of the sibling sets.

In the weeks after our first adoption conversation and the return from our cruise, we continued to pray for wisdom. The decision seemed so overwhelming that I ended up just pleading for a neon sign from God. I told Him I'd do whatever He wanted, even if it meant *not* adopting, but *I just needed to know.*

In the days after viewing the DVD, I continued to think about those four children. It seemed my thoughts would turn to them, especially as I drove, and I would spend time praying for them. I laugh now, remembering those first days when I couldn't remember how to pronounce Wendemagegn's name (Wind-a-mog-in). So my prayer was something like, "Dear God, be with Beza and, um, Wen—, um, whatever his name is."

(After a day or two of that, I stuck the DVD back in so I could imprint his name on my brain. Watching it made me cry again.)

More and more, my thoughts turned to Wendemagegn and Beza rather than the other sibling set.

On Friday, December 6, a rare rainy day in Phoenix, I was running errands during lunch. Like the last few days, I spent the quiet time thinking about Wendemagegn and Beza. Finally I said, "God, do you want us to adopt these kids?"

Clear as a bell, I heard a yes. Not audibly, but it was there—quick on the heels of my question. I had never experienced an answer from God that way. It was beautiful and thrilling at the same time.

But quickly the doubts began to sink in. I have an overactive imagination, and I can create whole "movies" in my head, imagining how a situation will turn out. What if my imagination just conjured up the answer I wanted to hear? I mean, I'd never heard God answer me like that, so what if it wasn't real? Fortunately, God knows about my thick skull; so He spoke to me again—just in a different way.

That afternoon I picked up Natalie from preschool and headed home. I took my normal freeway exit and sat in the left lane, ready to turn. I glanced over and on the right side, pulled off the road, sat a pickup truck with two older men in the bed holding a sign that said "Out of gas, please help."

In the same way I heard the yes earlier, I felt God tell me to give them $20. The light turned green and, somewhat annoyed, I moved over two lanes and turned right at the corner. The area is fairly rural, but there is a gas station on the corner; so I pulled in there. Then I realized that a four-foot chain link fence, thirty yards of overgrown grass, and a bit of a ditch separated me from the men. Plus it was still raining. There was no good way to get to them.

"Forget it. This is ridiculous," I said to myself, and I kept driving, swinging onto the road, headed home.

But the internal battle waged, and I heard God tell me to help them. I had driven probably one hundred yards when I turned and headed back—still slightly annoyed, I might add. This was really inconvenient after all.

Five-year-old Natalie piped up from the back, "Mommy, *what* are you doing?" She clearly thought I was crazy or lost.

I was still arguing with God as I pulled into the gas station. I circled around the pumps as it began to rain harder and tried once again to blow it off and leave. Wrong! I finally pulled up along the fence, got out in the rain, and headed toward the men.

One of them quickly jogged to the fence where I stood. I handed him the $20 bill with a half-hearted "God bless" and got in the van—my heart racing.

Despite my reluctance and my internal war, I knew as I drove home that God had issued that directive for one reason—to show me that the yes I heard earlier was from Him after all.

There was no denying it after that.

Throughout the adoption process, and even in our time since the kids have been home, my "gas station experience" has served as a great comfort to me. I have no doubt that God's plan was for Wendemagegn and Beza to be part of our family.

And so began our adoption journey.

CHAPTER ONE
THE ADOPTION ADVENTURE

If I could ask each one of you how you came to this place of adoption, I know your answers would be as varied as the places in which you live. For some of you the decision to adopt has come after years of struggling with infertility. Some may have one or more biological children but medical conditions make it impossible or unwise for you to have more children through birth. There are those who have biological children but now desire to grow their family through adoption because there are children who need families. You may have known you were going to someday adopt since you were a child. Or it may have completely taken you by surprise.

No matter how you got here, welcome to the grand adventure of adoption! And by *adventure* I don't mean a "Whee! I zip-lined through the jungles of Costa Rica" kind of adventure. I mean a "I climbed Mount Everest, got stuck at the top in a storm, wasn't sure I would survive, and then was told the only way down was via death-defying roller coaster" kind of adventure.

Adoption is beautiful. It is the quintessential picture of unconditional love. It will change you in a way very few other life experiences will. The process itself will challenge and grow you more than you could ever imagine. You will not be the same. Each of us has something to learn through this process. Something that God wants to teach us. For me it was a lesson in faith and giving God control. For you it might be something completely different.

There will never be a truer picture of love. To choose to love no matter the circumstances, no matter the background, no matter the future. Christ did it for us.

> But when the right time came, God sent his Son, born of a woman, subject to the law. God sent him to buy freedom for us who were slaves to the law, so that he could adopt us as his very own children. And because we are his children, God has sent the Spirit of his Son into our hearts, prompting us to call out, "Abba, Father." (Galatians 4:4-6)

Are you already imagining the day your adopted child will first call you "Mommy" or "Daddy?" Do you imagine the first time you will hold him or her, whether it's in a hospital on the day of birth or whether you meet inside the walls of an orphanage halfway around the world?

Adoption can seem exciting, perhaps even adventuresome, but it can also be overwhelming.

You may have seen astonishing numbers batted about—147 million orphans, 163 million orphans, 180 million.

It's difficult, of course, to be 100 percent accurate about the number of children who are orphans. Whether we're talking about numbers of 147 or 180 million orphans worldwide, it's important to understand the term *orphan* can mean different things.

With the U.S. foster care system there are over 100,000 children who are "orphaned." One or both of their birth parents may be living but the courts have deemed it in the best interest of the child to sever those parental rights and to work to find him or her a family. These children are waiting in temporary foster homes or group homes. Since 2002 an average of 53,000 children are adopted from foster care each year. Unfortunately, those numbers don't quite meet the demands when an average of 73,000 children have their parents' rights severed each year.[1] Sadly, some will remain orphans their entire life.

When speaking on a global scale, children can be classified as a "single orphan" (with one deceased parent) or a "double orphan" (no living parents). According to UNICEF and the United States government there are 153 million children worldwide who are orphans, but only 17.8 million of those are double orphans.[2]

Why is a child who has lost one parent considered an orphan? We don't tend to think in those terms in the United States. If Mark died and I were left to care for our four children alone, I don't think anyone would label them as orphans. Yes, our grief would be great, but we would still have housing, food, and medical care. My kids would continue to attend school, and I would be able to meet their financial needs. They would be provided for, protected, and nurtured.

However, in developing countries the death of a parent is a serious blow to the already fragile financial stability of the family. Approximately 60 percent of the world's orphans have lost their father, but have a surviving mother.[3] That family, like half the world, was already trying to survive on less than $2.50 a day.[4] The loss of the main income earner is devastating. How does a mom, often with no job skills or education, provide for and protect her children? One or more of her children may end up on the street fending for themselves. Or she may choose to place her younger children for adoption in hopes of giving them a better life.

When it is the mother who dies, cultural issues often come into play. In Ethiopia, for example, if a man remarries, the new wife will seldom accept the children from his previous marriage. At best they are tolerated, at worst they are abandoned and forced into orphanages or onto the streets. Even the reverse can be true. A stepdad may be less than welcoming to the children of his new wife.

In other countries, like China, gender issues are filling the orphanages with girls. Some say as many as a million girls are abandoned in China each year.[5] China's "One Child Policy," introduced in 1978, is often cast as the major cause of abandonment.

While the number of orphans grows larger, the number of international adoptions is decreasing. In 2012, only 8,668 children were adopted internationally by Americans, compared to nearly 23,000 in 2004.[6] International adoptions have been steadily decreasing for several years. China and Russia both instituted policy changes that slowed down adoptions in their respective countries. Then Russia shut down completely in 2013. Guatemala stopped new adoptions in late 2008 to allow time to establish more stringent guidelines after unethical practices were brought to light. Ethiopia showed an increase in the number of adoptions for several years, but that too will change since they announced a major slowdown in 2011.

Domestic infant adoptions are much harder to track because states are not required to report adoption numbers, and there is no central agency tracking the data. Best estimates put the number at approximately 18,000 infant adoptions per year. In the mid 1970s that number was closer to 49,000.[7] The decline can be attributed to a number of factors including access to contraception, decrease in stigma associated with single parenting, and the legalization of abortion.

Unfortunately, misconceptions and misinformation still abound. We often think of birth mothers as being young teenagers when in fact only about 25 percent are in their teens.[8] According to a study by the Evan B. Donaldson Adoption Institute, the most common situations for birth parents include:

- Women in their early to mid-twenties just launching their lives with a realistic understanding of the demand of parenting and the belief that they are unready.
- Single parents and occasionally married parents with other children. Women already struggling emotionally or financially often feel they cannot cope with parenting another child. They may be homeless, close to poverty, in the process of divorce, and so on.
- Teenagers who place their child for adoption are usually very goal-oriented and acknowledge they would not be a good parent at this point in their life.
- Women with extreme difficulties such as substance abuse, disabilities, poverty, or in situations of domestic violence may choose to voluntarily surrender their child rather than have them removed by the state.

- Victims of rape, either by relatives or strangers, may not feel emotionally able to parent the child.
- Young women from conservative backgrounds may feel shame and have no support. In some situations and cultures they may even fear for their safety if their pregnancy was discovered.
- Recent immigrants who may be undocumented and have no social support network.
- Parents expecting a baby with a disability.

For these women, the choice of adoption is vital. Knowing that they can choose to place their child with loving parents gives them an option other than abortion or parenting in circumstances they feel are not ideal.

The pro-life movement is now recognizing the importance of adoption and working to combat the stigma birth mothers may experience after placing their child for adoption. The 2014 March for Life in Washington, D.C., included James Dobson, founder of Focus on the Family, and his adopted son, Ryan, who encouraged adoption as an option for those facing an unwanted pregnancy.

The need is great but we seem to be on the cusp of a revolution—of couples, families, and single adults who are standing up to say, "Yes, I will make a difference. I will be a family for these children."

Many of them will walk the long, hard, often expensive road to adoption. But the truth is that many take one look at the cost of adoption and walk away, discouraged, believing they can never afford it.

Whether adoption is right for you is a complex decision, but the cost should not keep you from pursuing this dream. You can afford it without taking out a second mortgage or maxing out your credit cards. There are options—lots of them. *You Can Adopt Without Debt* helps bridge the gap for families who desire to adopt but need assistance with the financial aspect of making their dream a reality. Don't lose heart! Within these pages are helpful tips, tricks, and practical advice. Within these pages is hope.

CHAPTER TWO
WHAT TYPE OF ADOPTION
IS RIGHT FOR YOU?

If you've just begun to consider adoption, my guess is you're feeling pretty overwhelmed by the decisions that must be made. The Internet is a great research tool, but type in "adoption," and the 165 million results will make your eyes glaze over. The best advice? One step at a time.

Your first step is to decide what type of adoption to pursue. There are three main types to consider, each with its own set of benefits and potential drawbacks.

- Foster care adoption
- Domestic infant adoption
- International adoption

Before you proceed, take a few minutes to think about why you want to adopt and what that might look like for you. Jot down quick answers to the following questions.

- Do you want a newborn baby? Toddler? Older child?
- Is it important that the child have the same skin color as you?
- How much can you afford for your adoption? Are you willing or able to fund-raise or work overtime to pay for adoption?
- Are you open to adopting a child with special medical needs, either minor or major?
- Do you want to adopt a sibling group?

- Do you want to bring another culture into your family?
- Do you want to have continued contact with the child's birth family?
- How long are you willing to wait to adopt?
- Is knowing the child's family and medical history important?
- Are you willing to travel outside the country?

Have the answers to those questions in mind as you read this chapter. Your answers might change, but this list gives you a good starting framework.

Foster Care Adoption

There are over 104,000 children in foster care waiting to be adopted, ranging in age from less than one year old to twenty-one years of age.[1] It may seem strange to think of a twenty-one-year-old looking for a family, but this desire illustrates the importance of the love and security only a family can offer. Nearly 40 percent of foster children wait more than three years to be adopted.[2] During that time, they will likely live in multiple foster homes or possibly a group home.

Each year, at age eighteen, more than thirty thousand children age out of the U.S. foster care system, completely on their own.[3] Rarely have they been given the emotional support needed to make the transition. Many graduate without having learned basic life skills such as how to balance a checkbook or apply for a job. As a result, the rates of homelessness, crime, and drug abuse among these kids are high.

Unfortunately, stereotypes persist, and many people assume that children in the foster care system are juvenile delinquents.

The truth is that these children have been removed from their home through no fault of their own. Neglect, abuse, parental imprisonment, and death of a parent may land a child in the care of the state. Of course, it is almost impossible for these children not to have emotional scars. Even if they didn't suffer abuse or neglect, the solitary act of being removed from a parent's care is traumatic. But that trauma will reside in every child who is ever adopted, no matter what the circumstance and no matter his or her age. As a parent, you need to be willing to address these scars and accept them along with the child. Remember that biology does not guarantee a free pass when it comes to children's issues. Plenty of adoptive parents also deal with biological children whose issues mirror those of adopted kids.

Financially, foster care adoption is the least expensive way to adopt. Depending on the circumstances, these adoptions cost much less because expenses are paid by the state. In some cases there may be some small expenses but generally not more than $2,500. Many states offer extra incentives and subsidies to encourage foster adoption such as free healthcare for the child until adulthood or free in-state college tuition.

The initial goal with any child placed in foster care is, as it should be, to reunite the child with their parents if possible, or a relative. The government stipulates what changes the parents must make in order for reunification to happen. The plan for reunification may include substance abuse rehabilitation, parenting classes, or a change in living environment. The juvenile courts give the parents ample chances to meet those qualifications. For the 104,000 waiting children, the parents have failed to meet these stipulations and all parental rights have been terminated. There are over 200,000 more children who are in the system and somewhere in the reunification process.

Foster parents fall into two categories: those who specifically desire to provide temporary care during the reunification process and those specifically seeking to adopt from the foster system. Of course, *temporary* can still mean days, weeks, months, or even years. Foster parents might receive multiple placements of unrelated children at the same time, or sibling groups, or go through periods with no placements. Many of these parents get the opportunity to show love and support to dozens of children during their years of foster parenting. Really, this is a special ministry in and of itself.

For those interested in adoption from foster care, there are two options available. The first is to be matched with a waiting child who is legally available for adoption. Waiting children are the kids you see on sites like adoptuskids.org or featured on regular news segments local stations put together like "Wednesday's Child." The courts have already irrevocably severed the rights of their birth parents. The adoption process can still take one to two years depending on factors like training classes the state requires, your home study, and the time it takes to match you with a child.[4]

The second option is "foster-to-adopt." These children are still on a reunification plan but need a loving, stable family now. Of course, it is ideal for children to remain in one home until they are either adopted or reunited with parents or a relative who agrees to care for them. Being placed with a family that is licensed to foster and adopt is the best way to achieve a stable home environment.

Foster-to-adopt is not for the faint of heart but no type of adoption is without ups and downs. You could raise a child in your home for two years and have them returned to their birth parents, leaving you to start all over again. In reality, this could happen multiple times.

Foster mom Kelly Porter writes,

> You parent, and you love, and you wait for the foster system. While you love, more and more each day, you set to the side the reminders that you have absolutely and positively no control over the future of the little person in your care. You pray for forever, but social workers have a different job. In your mind you say there are no guarantees here, and you foolishly believe you have control over your heart, but you don't.[5]

So why choose foster-to-adopt? For starters, if you are hoping to adopt a younger child, under the age of three, you will most likely have to foster first. Second, this gives you a chance to make sure that your family is the right fit for the child. This may sound harsh but the reality is that sometimes these children have very specific needs. A child's past treatment and behavior may mean that he or she really needs to be placed in a household where he or she is an only child. There is often a "honeymoon" phase when a child first comes home.

Fostering allows time for things to normalize and for you to make sure you can meet the needs of the child.

Some states require foster parenting as the only way to adopt a child in the system.

Couples are often under the impression that adopting a young infant from the foster system is unheard of, but this is untrue. Many families are matched with newborns directly from the hospital. However, these infants will always initially be on the reunification path, so it may be a minimum of six months before they are available to adopt. Also, many babies are placed in foster care at birth because of exposure to alcohol or drugs in utero, and they may suffer the short-term or long-term effects.

In some cases, you may be able to maintain contact with your child's birth family and/or other siblings.

Pros

- Free or very inexpensive
- Possible continued financial support from the state

Cons

- Lengthy training process and possible lengthy matching process
- Uncertain future and possible "lost placements" when children go back to parents
- You may have to deal with difficult situations due to birth parent visitations during the fostering period
- Frustrating and sometimes confusing bureaucratic process

For more information, start at adoptuskids.org.

Domestic Infant Adoption

Many families desire the experience of parenting from birth without the uncertainty of bureaucracy involved in foster care. Domestic infant adoptions can be completed in a variety of ways, discussed more in chapter 4.

The average cost is $10,000 to $40,000 although various circumstances can push that figure higher.[6]

In a private domestic adoption, the matching process is primarily in the hands of the birth parents. Their agency or attorney may present them with several family profiles that meet the birth parents' criteria (geographic location, age, race, lifestyle, family size, and so on). The birth parents choose if they would like to meet with any potential adoptive parents and ultimately decide who will adopt their child.

Being matched with a birth mother is the greatest time variable in private adoption, but the average adoption is completed within two years.

Adoptive Families Magazine 2010–2011 Cost and Timing survey showed the following wait times between portfolio (family profile) completion and being matched with a birth mother.[7]

- Less than three months—33 percent
- Four to six months—17 percent
- Seven to twelve months—23 percent
- Thirteen to twenty-four months—18 percent
- Longer than twenty-four months—9 percent

Some parents are leery of private adoptions because birth parents have the right to change their mind at any point until the final consent papers are signed. Laws vary greatly by state, but there are currently only three states—Alabama, Hawaii, and Michigan—that allow birth mothers to legally consent to the adoption prior to the birth of the child. Even then, there are restrictions. In some cases, the birth father is able to sign consent earlier, but the other forty-seven states don't allow a birth mother to sign a final consent until the baby is born. In some cases, paperwork can be signed as soon as twelve hours after birth, but a few states require longer fifteen- to thirty-day waiting periods. Three days is the most common.[8] (Check your state adoption laws online.)

Birth parents do sometimes change their minds, either before the baby is born or immediately after. I don't think we can fully fathom how heartrending the decision to relinquish a child is unless we've been there ourselves. Thirty-eight percent of respondents to the Adoptive Families Cost and Timing survey worked with more than one birth mother before successfully completing an adoption.

However, the fear that a birth parent might come back years later and somehow gain custody of your adopted child is greatly unfounded. Consent to adopt is irrevocable unless obtained by fraud, duress, or undue influence. There is no hard data, but experts estimate that fewer than 1 percent of domestic adoptions are legally contested after parental rights have been terminated. Of course the media seizes on every one of these cases, which blows the fear way out of proportion.

Within a private adoption, the birth parents and adoptive family are free to decide if the adoption will be open, semi-open, or closed. Before 1970, nearly every private adoption was closed, and the records sealed by courts. Birth parents did not know any identifying information about the adoptive parents and vice versa. Today, only 5 percent of adoptions take place without some type of ongoing relationship between adoptive parents and birth parents.[9]

A semi-open adoption allows birth parents and adoptive parents to exchange non-identifying information, often through an intermediary. They may still meet face-to-face prior to the child's birth, but identifying details such as last names and hometown are kept private. Ongoing contact may include periodic pictures or letter exchanges done either through the attorney or agency or a private P.O. box. When the adopted child is of age and wants to make more direct contact with his or her birth parents, he or she may be given additional information from the courts or the adoption agency.

The details of an open adoption can vary greatly and the parameters are decided jointly between birth parents and adoptive parents. Often the relationship includes regular exchange of pictures and letters via mail or e-mail. It may even include periodic face-to-face visits with birth parents and/or other family members. Some parents of children through open adoption choose to graft members of the birth family into their extended family, including them for holidays, birthdays, and other special occasions.

A 2012 study by the Evan B. Donaldson Adoption Institute shows that open adoptions bring a greater satisfaction with the adoption process and that birth mothers report less grief, regret, and worry.[10] Adoptive parents often have a greater empathy toward birth parents, better communication with their child about their adoption, and a better relationship with their adopted child.

Some parents are drawn toward private, newborn adoption because they assume babies will not show the signs of trauma you might expect from kids adopted from foster care or internationally. This is a naive, but unfortunately widespread, belief. Admittedly, it was one I held until a year after we brought home our adopted kids.

I was at a one-day conference by Dr. Karyn Purvis, Director of the Institute of Child Development at Texas Christian University in Fort Worth, Texas. As the author of *The Connected Child*, Dr. Purvis is known as one of the foremost experts in parenting kids "from hard places."

Halfway through the morning, as Dr. Purvis explained how early trauma can affect brain development and the far-reaching effects, I found myself thinking, "But this sounds like Noah," my biological son who has ADHD, sensory integration disorder, and anxiety issues. Since he obviously hadn't ever been institutionalized, I was horrified to realize that our parenting must have done something to mess up his brain development.

I breathed a little easier as Dr. Purvis explained that trauma can come from many avenues. Being under an unusual amount of stress during pregnancy—say a career change, move, loss of a loved one—can affect the baby. When she explained that a medically traumatic birth can also have long-term effects on the baby, a light bulb went on.

Noah tied a knot in his umbilical cord at some point, so the last half of my twelve-hour labor was spent with me on oxygen and not moving for fear of cutting off his oxygen supply. When it came time to deliver, the doctor told me they were giving me twenty minutes to get him out before they delivered by C-section.

Fortunately, I was able to deliver quickly, but Noah still had some difficulty breathing. It was several hours before they released him to come see me in my room. After that, it was smooth sailing, so I never really thought about it again.

So imagine a birth mother who, even in the best of circumstances with a loving and supportive family, is making the hardest decision she will probably ever make in her life. To think that the stress of her situation will not affect her unborn child is unrealistic.

Even if the birth mother chooses to never hold her child, the brain chemistry and chemical bond between mother and child is deeply rooted. Did you know that infants can even tell the difference between their mother's breast milk and that of another woman?[11] Even if they go straight from delivery into the waiting arms of an adoptive mom who has prepared herself to lactate, that baby still intrinsically knows the difference. Why? Because God created our bodies in such a miraculous way that the umbilical fluid the child has been nurtured in contains the same "flavor" as the mother's breast milk. How cool is that?

But the miracle of God's creative design is that those tiny brains can heal, adapt, and bond to the adoptive parents with the proper love and parenting techniques. This holds true for older kids as well. Dr. Karyn Purvis makes it a point to tell adoptive parents that she has never seen a child from trauma that couldn't heal.

Pros

- Able to adopt newborns
- Better knowledge of medical history and background of birth parents
- Possible continued relationship with birth family

Cons

- Uncertain wait time dependent on matching process
- Possible disappointment of birth parents changing their minds
- Average cost $20,000 to $40,000. Difficult to predict your exact cost before beginning

For more information, start at theadoptionguide.com.

International Adoption

International adoption may seem to get all the media attention, but in truth, it happens in smaller numbers than both foster care and private adoptions.

Several high-profile celebrity adoptions have shined the spotlight on international adoption, and you'd be a rare international adoptive parent if at least one person hasn't asked you if you adopted because Angelina Jolie did it. As if she were the pioneer.

While international orphan numbers are staggering, only a small percentage of those children will ever be eligible for international adoption and an even smaller number get adopted each year. In 2012, 8,668 children were adopted internationally by U.S. citizens.[12]

Over 92 percent of international adoptions are from only twenty countries with China, Ethiopia, Russia, South Korea, and Ukraine being the top five in 2012 and accounting for 71 percent of adoptions.[13] Russia has since closed adoptions to the United States. The Philippines, India, Colombia, Uganda, and Taiwan rank fifth through tenth in international adoptions.

Each country has specific requirements for international adoption that cover the potential parent's age, marital status and length of marriage, income, residency, and other details.

For example, to adopt from China both parents must be between the ages of thirty and fifty. Only heterosexual couples who have been married at least two years are qualified. If either party was previously divorced then the current marriage must be at least five years in length. Single women may adopt special needs children. They must have income equal to $10,000 per family member (including the adopted child) and have no major health issues or a body mass index over forty. China has one of the longer lists of requirements.

The U.S. State Department website on intercountry adoption provides a detailed list of adoption requirements for each country and is the best place to look for details on adopting from a specific country (travel.state.gov).

All international adoptions must follow the process set forth by both the United States and the country from which you are adopting. That process determines three things: (1) the parents are deemed suitable to adopt, (2) the child meets their birth country's criteria for adoption, and (3) the child's adoption meets the requirements to immigrate to the United States.

In 1994, the United States became part of the Hague Adoption Convention, an international agreement designed to safeguard intercountry adoptions and eliminate corruption. If you are adopting from a Hague Convention country, you must use a Hague-accredited agency to complete your home study and adoption. Of the top ten countries for international adoption, only four are Hague countries as of 2013—China, Philippines, India, and Colombia.

While extra rules and regulations may slow down the process somewhat, Potential Adoptive Parents (PAPs) must understand that these requirements are a good thing. It is a small sacrifice to make to know that both birth parent rights and child rights are being protected.

Time lines for international adoption can be as short as one year or as long as five years. Adopting a healthy, young girl from China puts you in that five-year line. Adopting an older child with special needs can shorten the time period dramatically.

Some parents lean toward international adoption because they think it's more of a "sure thing"—they don't have to wait to be chosen by a birth mother only to possibly have her change her mind. The birth parents will never come back and try to claim the child.

But in truth, international adoption has its own pitfalls. Yes, once you sign with an agency, you are pretty much guaranteed a child, and usually you are given a fairly accurate time frame. But sometimes things happen.

Adoption agencies can shut their doors with little or no notice. In February 2013, two adoption agencies, Christian World Adoption and Adoption Ark, suddenly closed their doors and declared bankruptcy. Families in the process of adopting through these agencies lost any money they had already paid to the agency and had no choice but to start over with a new agency if they still wanted to adopt. Christian World Adoption had been operating for more than twenty years.

When working with any foreign government, there is an element of unpredictability. When Russia announced a ban on adoptions to U.S. citizens in December 2012, it left three hundred families who had already been matched and who had met their adoptive children in limbo. The majority of those cases are still unresolved. The Democratic Republic of Congo temporarily suspended adoptions while it worked out some of its processes in-country. This increased wait times and even caused several families in-country to pick up their children only to get stuck there for an extended period of time.

Tragedies can also happen. Occasionally, a child will die after being matched with an adoptive family. (This is more likely to happen with very young babies who come into care of the orphanage already in poor health or children with special needs.) Sometimes a relative does show up and agree to care for the child you've been matched with.

This information is not to scare you off, but it is important that you approach any adoption armed with as much information as possible.

Shortly after my husband and I were matched with Wendemagegn and Beza, our caseworker gave me a great piece of advice. "Love them, but hold them with open hands," she said. I knew that I would do everything in my power to bring them home, but I also tried to remember that I was not in control. Fortunately, I knew that Christ, who loved them far more than I ever could, had it all in His hands.

Pros

- Timeline is generally known and predictable
- Child has already been relinquished with little possibility of a birth parent changing his or her mind
- Cost is known and, except for some rare exceptions, doesn't change unexpectedly
- You get to travel to and experience your adoptive child's birth country

Cons

- Little to no family/medical history will be known
- Institutionalized care can cause developmental delays and increased problems in attachment
- Infants will generally be at least six months of age or older before arriving home.
- Average cost $30,000 to $50,000

For more information, start at travel.state.gov.

Embryo Adoption

There is a fourth kind of adoption that is not necessarily an option for everyone but deserves mentioning. Embryo adoption, a growing trend in the last five years, is an option for adoptive couples where the woman is medically capable of carrying a baby to full term. In a case where infertility stems from the husband's medical issues, embryo adoption is a viable option.

Many couples, after going through one or more successful in vitro fertilization (IVF) treatments, may have embryos remaining. They couple has three options—discard them, donate them to embryonic stem cell research, or donate them to another couple.

Legally the term *adoption* refers to the placement of a child after birth, so embryo adoption is actually a legal agreement transferring the "property" of the embryos from the genetic parents to the adopting

parents. Because of this, embryo adoption is not eligible for the adoption tax credit.

For more information on embryo adoption, look at the National
Embryo Donation Center or Nightlight Christian Adoptions.

Making the Decision

So now what? How do you decide which type of adoption to pursue? Of course the decision should be made after much prayer and
discussion.

If you are married, it is vital you and your spouse are on the same
page. If you are not on the same page, be patient. It is not uncommon
for one half of a couple to be the initial champion of adoption. If this
is the case, and your spouse is not fully on board, don't push or rush.
Allow him or her time to process everything. Ask what is causing the
hesitation. What are his or her fears? Your spouse may be concerned
with the cost or wonder if he or she could love an adopted child as
much as biological children. It's a very big decision!

Wait, pray, keep talking about it. If this is God's plan for your family, He will bring your spouse around in His timing. Later, when the
tough times come, and they will, having a spouse who felt pushed
into adoption would make things infinitely harder on your relationship as your new family takes shape.

If you are single, find a trusted friend or family member to be your
sounding board and help you process all the information you are
learning.

Go back to the questions at the beginning of the chapter. Have any
of your answers changed? Rank them in order of importance.

One family might desire a low-cost adoption and be open to wide
age ranges and sibling groups. For them, foster care adoption might
be the right answer.

Others might feel drawn to adopting outside their culture and are
willing to wait longer and afford a more costly adoption.

A couple that has struggled with infertility may really desire a newborn and, therefore, turn to private, domestic adoption.

There is no one right answer. Undoubtedly, you will encounter people who have very strong opinions on adoption. I've been asked at least a dozen times, "Why did you adopt internationally when there are children right here in the U.S. who need homes?" What rankles me is (1) the person asking is usually doing nothing to help kids in the U.S. and (2) it implies that children in Africa are less worthy than American children.

And it is equally as good that some people do want to adopt infants because if there were no families wanting to adopt newborn babies, women with crisis, unplanned pregnancies would have only two options—abortion or raising a child when they feel they couldn't. Each family must choose for themselves the right situation. Every child is created in God's image and deserves a loving family. Let God lead you to the child or children He has for your family.

CHAPTER THREE
CHOOSING AN AGENCY OR ATTORNEY

Once you've decided what type of adoption to pursue, your next big obstacle is selecting an agency or, in the case of domestic adoptions, an attorney.

Foster Care Adoption

It may seem obvious that your adoption is handled through the state you reside in. But, in fact, a lot of states contract with several different agencies to provide services to children in foster care. Some may be run by your city or county, but some will be private agencies. Search "foster care licensing agencies" and your city/state. Just in my county alone there are nineteen licensing agencies. If you have choices, it is important that you find an agency that fits your family.

If you know other foster parents, ask them for recommendations or insight on agencies they have worked with. If you don't, then your best bet is to work the phones. Call each agency and make notes, not just of their answers, but they way you are treated.

Some initial questions:

- How often do they hold orientation meetings? When is the next one?
- Do they charge any fees for their services? If so, how much and what are they for?
- What requirements do they have above what the state requires?
- What age children do they typically place?

- Do they work with families like yours? (that is, number of other children, size of home, any other things you may wonder about.)
- How many hours of training are required annually?
- If applicable to you, ask what their philosophy is on placing infants with working parents.

When you have narrowed down the list, attend orientation meetings for all the agencies you felt comfortable with. At the meeting make note of the following things:

- Did you feel welcomed, comfortable, and respected?
- Was the information presented clear, detailed, and realistic?
- Did the staff speak about the children and birth families respectfully?
- Did you hear from experienced parents who adopted through the agency?
- What kind of support services will be available after a child is placed in your home? What about after the adoption is final?
- Do you and the agency have similar religious/social values?
- Did they make everything seem rosy and easy? Or did they overemphasize the negative? You want a balance between realism and enthusiasm.
- Do they help arrange "respite care" and if so, what are their requirements for care providers? (Respite care is sporadic child care reimbursed by the state. It allows foster parents a respite from the demands of caring for kids who sometimes require a little more attention. Depending on the parental reunification plan, foster children may also not be allowed to go out of the state. In the case that the rest of the family is traveling, respite care provides a place for the foster child to go during that time. Official respite care workers are trained and licensed by the state. Find out in what circumstances your babysitters need to be licensed.)

- How often do they do home visits? Full home inspections?
- Were you invited to follow up with the staff if you have more questions? Did they quickly answer your calls or do you have to leave voice mails?
- If you leave messages, do they return them in a timely manner?
- No matter what, *always* talk with other families who have used that agency. They should be happy to provide you with names and contact information for references.

Domestic Infant Adoption

Within domestic infant adoption there are two types—agency and independent. However, only forty-six states allow independent adoptions, and the regulations differ within those states.[1] (Colorado, Connecticut, Delaware, and Massachusetts don't allow independent adoptions.) Your state adoption laws regulate several other things, including: who may adopt, who must consent and when they can do it, regulation of expenses, use of advertising and facilitators, access to adoption records, and how to resolve paternity issues.

Find out what your specific state adoption laws are. The U.S. Department of Health and Human Services maintains the Child Welfare Information Gateway (CWIG), which contains a wealth of information, including a state statues search at childwelfare.gov /systemwide/laws_policies/state/. Under "Who May Place a Child for Adoption" you will find your choices. For example in Arizona, my home state, it says:

A child may be placed as follows:

- The child's birth or adoptive parent may consent to a direct placement or an agency placement.
- A licensed child-placing agency or the Department of Economic Security may handle a direct placement or an agency placement.
- A state-licensed attorney may handle direct placements.

Agency adoptions must be done in partnership with an agency licensed to work in your state. Again, the CWIG website contains a National Foster Care and Adoption Directory listing private and public agencies in every state. However, it is important to note that the larger nationwide agencies, such as Bethany Christian Services, are not listed here, just agencies physically located in your state. If you are looking at working with a nationwide agency, first contact them and make sure they are able to work with you. (If they can, and are located out of state, you will need to find a home study provider licensed in your state to complete that portion of your adoption.)

Adoption agencies may be either for-profit or nonprofit. That designation has more to do with their tax and legal matters and does not necessarily dictate whether they will be less expensive or whether they are more ethical. Agencies that have a religious affiliation may only work with people of a certain faith, or they may be open to all applicants. Again, don't assume that a religious agency is more ethical than a public agency. You must still do your research.

The main advantage to using an agency is that they take on the work of finding birth mothers. Most agencies spend thousands of dollars advertising their services to birth mothers locally or across the nation through print, broadcast, and online media. On the one hand, that saves you the expense and work of doing it yourself and may provide a faster match. But it also means that you are at the mercy of the agency. They select which birth mothers see your portfolio.

Adoption agencies usually also provide services to the birth mom and/or dad in the area of counseling and support. This is crucial and definitely something you want to look for. An ethical agency wants the birth parents to make the right decision for them. At the same time they also want to protect the rights of the adoptive parents. Talk to the agency about how they make sure both sides receive quality care during the process.

The list of options can seem overwhelming so, again, you may want to start with personal referral. Do you know anyone in your state who has adopted an infant? If so, ask which agency they used or if they know of good ones. You might also search for adoptive family groups in your state on both Facebook and within Yahoo Groups and then ask them as well. There is a Yahoo Group titled "Adoption Agency Research—Domestic" (groups.yahoo.com/neo/groups/AARD/info) where prospective adoptive parents can get feedback on specific agencies.

Most adoptive parents are more than willing to share about their story. Remember though, as you're listening to their story, that adoption is a complicated process and is rarely completely smooth. But, were they happy with how their agency dealt with bumps encountered along the way? Was anything unethical going on?

As you conduct your research, you can narrow your choices by deciding things like whether you want to work with a local agency or a national one. Do you want a small (fewer adoptions each year) or large agency? How many years of experience do you want the agency to have? Do they work in your state? Do you meet the age, marital status, gender selection, financial, and religious requirements of the agency?

Once you have a manageable list of agencies to research further, work through the list of questions below. You may find a lot of the answers on the agency website but make sure you also take time to speak with someone on the phone.

- How long have you been in business?
- How many staff do you have? On average, how long have they been with the agency?
- Are any of your staff adoptive parents? What level of education do most of your staff have?
- How many children were placed last year?
- How many adoptive parents are you currently working with?
- How do you find expectant mothers who may be considering adoption?

- What type of counseling do you offer to the birth parents (both pre-adoption and post-adoption)? Is it free to them? How many of your birth parents use your counseling services?
- How long after I apply will my home study begin? How long will it take?
- What is the average wait time from home study approval to referral? (If possible, be specific to your type of adoption—age, marital status, other children, race, and so on)
- What is the total cost for adopting? Can I get a written breakdown of the fees and when each fee is due?
- What expected expenses aren't listed on the agency fees?
- What is your refund policy if we change our minds or switch to an independent adoption?
- Who pays for the expectant mother's medical costs?
- Who pays for the expectant mother's living expenses and what is allowable by state law?
- Do we receive a refund or credit if a match falls through after we have paid fees or expenses?
- Do you facilitate compliance with the Interstate Compact on the Placement of Children if we adopt a child from another state? How much experience do you have with this Interstate Compact?
- What happens if we find a birth mother from another source? Will you complete the adoption? What if the birth mother doesn't want to do an agency adoption? Will any of my money be refunded? Or can it be applied to a later second adoption?
- What kind of training do you require for adoptive parents? Do you provide it or must we find it on our own? How many hours are required? Is it in-person or are there online options?
- Do you have support groups for adoptive parents?
- What post-adoption services do you offer—counseling, education, reunions?
- What percentage of your birth mothers choose to do an open adoption? How do you facilitate open adoptions?

- How do you communicate with prospective adoptive parents? Will we have one caseworker assigned to us? How many cases does he or she have at one time?
- Do you have a policy to return phone calls and e-mails within a set amount of time?
- What are your office hours?

Again, it's not just the answers to the questions, but the way you were treated when you talked with the agency. Were they easy to talk with? Did they seem knowledgeable and patient answering all of your questions? Were they clear and up-front about costs and what to expect or did they try to paint a rosy picture?

Independent adoptions are done when the birth parents and adoptive parents find each other and then proceed through the adoption with the help of an adoption attorney. Remember, independent adoptions are not legal in Colorado, Connecticut, Delaware, and Massachusetts. A knowledgeable adoption attorney will help you navigate the specific regulations your state law requires for independent adoptions.

Your attorney's job is to explain your adoption options and the laws that apply. He or she will obtain the birth parents' medical history as well as any prenatal medical records to be evaluated by the adoptive parents and their doctor. They will determine what birth mother costs are permissible for you to pay, and ensure that the birth parents' rights are legally terminated before the adoption placement is finalized. The attorney also helps both parties reach an agreement about whether the adoption will be closed, open, or semi-open and draft an agreement to ensure the best interests of all parties. Depending on the size of the firm, they may or may not provide counseling to birth parents.

Adoption law is a very specialized field so hiring the same lawyer who helped your write your will or close a real estate deal is not advised. Hire an adoption attorney. Some lawyers and law firms specialize solely in adoption; others also work in other areas of family law—paternity, custody, divorce. Ask what percentage of their cases are adoptions and look for someone whose practice is at least 50 percent adoption.

As with agencies, the first thing you should do is ask around. If you know someone who has adopted, ask for attorney references. Second, the American Academy of Adoption Attorneys (adoptionattorneys. org) maintains a list based on geographic location. Review their websites and phone to ask some general questions such as:

- How many nonrelative adoption cases have they handled?
- What is their average placement time?
- What extended services do they offer birth parents, such as counseling?

If you have to leave messages, take note of how quickly they return your calls.

While some private adoption attorneys actively seek out prospective birth parents, many ask that the adoptive parents shoulder this responsibility. They may provide assistance and advice on how to find a birth mother or you may be completely on your own. Adoptive parents may use personal networking, the Internet, and traditional print advertising to appeal to expectant mothers considering adoption. There are also adoption consultation services that can help with all or parts of your journey.

When you've narrowed down your list, interview at least a couple attorneys to find one you feel comfortable with. Most offer a free or very low-cost initial consultation. In order to determine if you like the attorney and feel comfortable, be sure to ask lots of questions. Find out how much he or she charges and whether it is a flat fee or an hourly rate. Be certain to ask what other expenses you will incur such as filing fees, their mileage costs, and so on. Even if he or she charges an hourly rate, the attorney should be able to give you a fairly good estimate of your costs. Remember that a more experienced lawyer may charge more per hour, but they may also take fewer hours to do the work than a less-experienced lawyer.

Many lawyers require an up-front retainer fee. This is deposited and used as a credit for your expenses. Once the lawyer's time and expenses exceed that initial retainer, your statements will indicate a balance due. Determine how much their retainer fee is and what happens to it if the birth mother changes her mind. Ask how often the lawyer will send you an accounting statement and how detailed it will be.

International Adoption

Finding the right international adoption agency begins with deciding from which country you plan to adopt. Not every agency operates programs in all countries. If you're adopting from China, Ethiopia, Ukraine, or South Korea, you will have more options than if you are adopting from some place like Honduras.

As with the other types of adoptions, a good place to start is always with personal referrals. Who do you know that's adopted from the same country? If no one, reach out to any international adoption parents you know and ask if they know anyone who has adopted from the country you're interested in. Ask them to connect you via Facebook or e-mail so you can ask questions.

There are several online avenues to do research and read reviews on adoption agencies, including:

- Yahoo Group "The Adoption Agency Research Group" (groups.yahoo.com/neo/groups/Adoption_Agency_Research /info)
- Adoption Agency Ratings—adoptionagencyratings.com
- Adoption Agency Reviews—adoptionagencyreviews.com
- Guidestar (for nonprofit agencies)—guidestar.org
- Better Business Bureau—bbb.org

Keep in mind there will *always* be people who are unhappy and have complaints. Adoption is a roller coaster with many variables that render it unpredictable—international adoption especially so.

Some people have completely unrealistic expectations and their complaints will reflect that. So as you hear from others, you need to filter through the comments and look for the valuable insights.

You do not need to work with an agency located in your state. In fact, odds are you won't. As long as your home-study provider is licensed in your state, it does not matter where your adoption agency is physically located. Most of your correspondence is going to be done via phone and e-mail regardless.

It is important to note that individual adoption agencies often place their own requirements on top of the country requirements. This can be quite confusing. When we first began our research, I received information from one of the large national agencies that said you could not adopt from Ethiopia if you had a history of mental illness and had ever been prescribed medication for depression. I thought we were out of the game because I have a history of depression. Then I realized that it was an agency requirement, not a regulation of the Ethiopian government even though the agency literature made it sound otherwise. Our family also didn't meet the income guidelines of some agencies that required you to have $10,000 in income per person in the family, even though the Ethiopia government has no such minimum. If you don't meet one agency's extra requirements, move on to the next one on your list.

There are cost differences between agencies, but I would caution that this should not be your primary factor in choosing an agency. Cheaper isn't always better, especially in the international adoption world. Especially if there is a huge cost difference. Why are they cheaper? Are they smaller and only focus on one or two countries so they have fewer staff and less expenses? Are their costs subsidized by donations? A few agencies do offer a sliding scale for their fees based on family income.

Ethics, however, should be a large part of your decision-making process. Not that ethics are unimportant in domestic and foster adoptions, but international adoption is a field rife with ethical concerns.

With the potential for large amounts of money coming into developing countries, international adoption can become a magnet for corruption.

Many Prospective Adoptive Parents (PAPs) assume that children available for international adoption have no living birth parents or were abandoned with no further trace of their birth families. The reality is much more complicated and the truth is that, unfortunately, there are cases of impoverished birth families being deceived, coerced, or even paid to give up their children for adoption.

Unfortunately it is stories like these that often lead to the suspension or cessation of international adoption in different countries. Guatemala is a perfect example. Before it closed international adoption in 2008, there was little oversight and approximately one in every one hundred ten children born were being adopted by Americans. The majority of these adoptions went through private attorneys who charged outrageous fees and handled everything from terminating the birth parents' rights to choosing the adoptive family. And for the most part it was not the children waiting in institutionalized care who were being adopted. It was healthy young children who had living birth parents.[2]

It is too easy for adoptive parents to be made the priority when the priority should always be the children. What is best for them? An ethical adoption agency will always put the best interests of the child in the forefront. Author and adoptive mother Jen Hatmaker wrote two great blog posts on the ethics of international adoption, which I urge you to read: "Examining International Adoption Ethics," parts 1 and 2. She said, "The best we can do…is take a high view of adoption and insist on ethical practices, transparency, and a commitment to help and not hurt."[3]

As with foster and domestic adoption you will want to ask a lot of questions of any agency you are exploring and pay attention to how they treat you and how you get along with the staff. In addition to the questions listed in the sections above, ask the following:

- Is the agency accredited and? (In its state, and in the country you want to adopt from.) Has its license ever been suspended?
- How long has it been in business?
- How long has it facilitated adoptions from this country?
- What are their minimum requirements for adopting from country X?
- How many children were placed from country X in the last year? How many were special needs children? How many were older than age five?
- What is the average wait time for a family adopting from country X and requesting a child in the age range you want?
- What type of pre-adoption training is required?
- What post-adoption services do they offer?
- Will they provide references of families who have adopted from country X?
- What happens if there are changes to the country program and adoptions are shut down or stalled? Can you switch to another country without losing any of your fees?
- Do they have direct links to programs in the country such as orphanages and child welfare agencies? Or do they rely on intermediaries to find and match children?
- Does the agency have staff members in-country? If so, how long have they been with the agency and how are they paid? (It is preferable to have workers who are paid a fixed salary versus per adoption for obvious reasons.)
- Who determines that the children are appropriate for adoption? If this is someone outside the agency's staff, does the agency also verify the child's background?
- If the children have living birth parents are you allowed to interact with them? If yes, can you bring our own independent translator?
- Does the agency have orphan prevention and family reunification programs in place?

- Outside of adoption, what programs or support do they operate in the countries where they work?
- What type of support do they provide to parents who are traveling?

When traveling internationally, agency staff will often assist with translation issues. However, if you have the opportunity to visit with any of your child's extended family, I would recommend taking an independent translator that you hire on your own. This helps avoid "selective translating" and assures that you can have a truthful and honest conversation. Use this time to ask about the child's history but in a sensitive way. Think about what your child will want to know about his or her family. What were their parents like? What jobs did they have? How did they meet each other? Where was your child born? What special memories does the family have of the child? What extended family are still living?

CHAPTER FOUR
WHAT TO EXPECT IN THE PROCESS

While it is impossible to account for every nuance of the different types of adoptions and country processes, this chapter provides a general overview so you know what to expect.

Once you decide on the type of adoption you will pursue and choose an agency or attorney, the first major step will be to complete your home study.

Home Study

A home study serves several purposes:

- To evaluate the fitness of the Prospective Adoptive Parents (PAPs) for adoption
- To educate and prepare the PAPs
- To provide adoption professionals such as your social worker, agency, and attorneys an in-depth understanding of your family's unique characteristics in order to ensure the best fit for the child(ren) placed in your home, and to ensure the most successful outcome.

Home study requirements vary by state, by agency, and by country if adopting internationally. If adopting from a Hague Convention country, additional home study requirements must be met.

The home study is written by a social worker licensed in your state. If you are working with an agency based out of another state (quite common in international adoption), they may assign you a local agency to complete your home study. If this option is available to you, ask around and look for recommendations from other adoptive families. If you have your choice of social workers, find one you like. You will be interacting with him or her for years to come.

The home study is your introduction to everyone's favorite part of adoption—*paperwork*! You will complete an in-depth application that will include:

Medical information—Usually the PAPs will be required to have a physical and a doctor's statement of good health. If you have children or other adults living in the home, they may need a physical as well. Aside from serious health issues that would affect your life expectancy, being under a doctor's care for an ongoing condition such as diabetes should not affect your approval. If you have a history of treatment for mental illness, be prepared to provide more information, but don't assume it will eliminate you.

Income Statements—You must verify your income by providing W-2s or paystubs as well as providing information on savings, investments, life insurance policies, and debts.

Background Check—Every state requires a background and fingerprint check. Don't assume that a young adulthood scrape with the law will disqualify you for adoption, but be open with your social worker. He or she wants to know how you handled the situation, what you learned from it, and how it may affect your parenting. Above all, be *honest*. If it is discovered later that you were deceptive, the consequences can be worse than if you had just been truthful.

Autobiographical Statement—Even though he or she does multiple interviews with you, the best way for the social worker to get to know you is by reading your autobiographical statement. Start by describing your life growing up, your education, your career, your marriage, any children you have, your neighborhood, your church, and so on. Your social worker may provide an outline or list of questions for you to work from.

References—Your agency will want three to four references from adults who know you extremely well. They may allow one of these to be related to you, but close friends, a pastor, or employer are also good sources. The social worker might give you a specific form to send to your chosen references or just collect names and addresses and contact them independently. Be sure to select people who will follow through and return the reference form or social worker's call promptly.

Supporting Paperwork—You need certified copies of birth certificates for every person living in your house, as well as your marriage license if you are married. If either spouse has been divorced, get certified copies of divorce decrees. You may also need to provide shot records for pets, copies of life insurance policies, and proof that you have a guardianship plan in place for your children should something happen to both parents.

Tip: When getting certified copies of birth certificates, licenses, and so on, get multiple copies. You will need them.

The social worker will interview you several times during your home study. The initial interview may take place at his or her office, but at least one interview will be in your home during the home visit. Married couples are interviewed together and separately.

During the interviews, the social worker will ask about your experiences with children, your parenting style, important relationships, your marriage, your childhood, and so on. If you have struggled with infertility, the social worker will want to know how you have handled the associated loss and grief. Parts of the process will seem like a job interview—describe your strengths and weaknesses, and so on. Again, be honest and open. No one is expecting perfection.

The home visit allows the social worker to get to know your family and ensure the environment is safe for a child. Somehow, PAPs usually translate this into a mad cleaning session, the likes of which your house may never have seen before. Trust me when I say that no social worker is concerned about dust bunnies under your bed. A normal cleaning suffices. You will not be judged on the style of your décor or the newness of your furniture, so there is no need to feel insecure. Your maintenance of a clean and safe home is all your social worker cares about.

Safety is the biggest concern. Your social worker will look for functioning smoke alarms, restricted pool access, firearm storage and security, and safe, out-of-reach storage for household cleaners, medicines, and sharp objects like knives. The child's room doesn't need to be ready for move-in, but do show the social worker where the new family member will sleep.

Social workers have walked this road with dozens, usually hundreds of families, so take advantage of their expertise. During our home visit, our social worker was helpful in deciding sleeping arrangements. We initially planned to have the girls share a room but give Wendemagegn his own room, mostly because our biological son has some trouble sleeping and can be quite particular about his things and space. We thought it might make the transition smoother. She reminded us that most likely both children were used to sharing one big room with several people and that Wendemagegn might be more comfortable sharing a room—at least for a while.

That arrangement is still in place over five years later. While a shared bedroom does sometimes present sleep challenges for the boys, they have experienced some definite good brother bonding (that is, wrestling and goofing off) after lights out.

If you are adopting from foster care, your home visit may go deeper and be classified as a home inspection. I know at least one family who has had the temperature in their refrigerator checked. Get a list of requirements from your social worker so you know ahead of time what the requirements are.

Your social worker will ask why you want to adopt and what age child you think might be best for your family. He or she will also, if applicable, talk with you about what kind of a relationship you hope to continue with the child's birth family.

Part of your social worker's job is to ensure that you are not approaching this process naively. Most PAPs, at one point or another, will wonder if the social worker is trying to scare them off. The answer is yes, sort of. No one likes to think that the worst-case scenario will happen to them, but you must. Part of a social worker's job is to ensure that you have thought through the more common difficulties and even the scarier ones: sibling rivalry, sleep issues, behavioral problems, attachment disorders, and even sexual abuse or inappropriateness.

During the home study, you must decide how many children you are interested in adopting and what, if any, special needs you are open to parenting.

Some families, despite leaning toward adopting just one child, request approval for two, leaving the possibility open for a sibling group or even two unrelated children. I know more than one family who fully intended to only adopt one child but was extremely glad they left room for flexibility when God led them to a second child during their process. It was much easier than getting their home study revised and reapproved.

Many social workers have firsthand experience, having adopted or been adopted themselves. They have also seen a lot during their years. Use their wisdom to help you.

On the other hand, realize a social worker may also be biased in some areas. For example, some are against adopting out of birth order or placing older teens in families with young children. Some families who held different views than that of their social worker have had to be persistent in expressing their desires to ensure that their social worker respected their position. This might mean a conference with multiple representatives from their agency. It might be a good idea to ask how the social worker feels about your potential adoption situation before you hire him or her.

Remember, your social worker is required to approve your family to adopt within certain parameters, and you will not be approved for any child who falls outside of those parameters. So, if you feel strongly that you are willing and able to parent, let's say, a child with special needs and your social worker disagrees, you have options. But do the research, be well prepared to state your case as to why you disagree, and do so with tact.

Thankfully God gave us the social worker He knew was right for our family. One who made sure we understood the risks and were making an educated decision.

After the interviews are complete, the social worker writes your home study report. The entire process can take three to six months. The completed home study will be the primary document used by your agency to help match you with a child and, if you are adopting internationally, will go in your dossier.

Dossier / Portfolio

Concurrently with the home study process, you can begin working on your dossier (international adoptions) or portfolio (domestic, newborn adoptions).

Dossier is a fancy word for a giant stack of paperwork that goes to the foreign government of your child's country. A *portfolio* is the photo book that prospective birth mothers will read to first meet your family.

Dossier

The process of compiling the information for your dossier can be overwhelming, but if you stay organized and tackle one thing at a time, it can come together quite quickly. You may want to purchase an expanding folder organizer or a three-ring binder with folders or plastic sleeves to keep everything organized.

Check with your agency, but most of your dossier documents, if they are not already certified copies, need to be notarized. Your bank or your employer may provide free notary services. Many companies have at least one notary on staff. If you need to get a health statement notarized and your doctor does not have a notary in the office (most don't), you can hire a mobile notary to come to the office. Most agencies suggest that you make sure the notary's commission does not expire earlier than a year from the current date because your documents need to be valid through the waiting period. This is a good time to mention that if your adoption process takes several years, you will likely have to update some of your documents along the way to keep them current.

The contents of a dossier are specific to your adoptive country and your agency, but the following list will give you a basic idea of what to expect. Your agency may have specific forms to use for doctor reports, references, and so on.

Personal Paperwork
- For married parents: certified copies of birth and marriage certificates
- For single parents: certified copy of birth certificate
- Certified copy of divorce decree (if applicable)
- Certified copy of death certificate of former spouse (if applicable)
- Financial information—Written letters from your bank stating your account balances
- Health Statement—Written report by your physician (on his or her letterhead) after your physical
- Proof of home ownership or rental agreement
- Employment verification—Ask your company's human resources department for a letter stating how long you have worked for the company along with your current annual salary. It must be on company letterhead. (Note: You must include employment verification even if you are self-employed.)
- Copy of the photo pages of your passport. If you don't have one yet, start that process now as it can take several months.
- Letters of reference—It's OK to use the same people you used for references for your home study
- Most recent federal income tax return
- Photographs of your family, relatives, pets, and house

Agency / Government Paperwork
- Adoption petition provided by your agency.

- Post Placement Agreement provided by your agency. This document testifies that you will do regular post-placement reports per the country's requirements. For us, that meant having our social worker visit at three, six, and twelve months after bringing the kids home. After that, we write and submit a report to the Ethiopian government once a year until the kids turn eighteen.
- Power of Attorney—Your agency will have a form. This allows them to act on your behalf in the adoption process.
- Form I-171H from the USCIS—You receive this after filing an I-600A form (See "Obtaining an Immigrant Visa" below).
- Home study report provided by your social worker.
- License of your adoption agency—provided by your agency.
- Criminal background check obtained from your local police station. You will need one for each parent. If you have other adults in the home (grandmother, child over eighteen), you may need to include one for them as well. Check with your agency.

There are dossier compilation services available that will do the bulk of the work for you if you want to pay the extra fee of $800 to $1,000 on top of the normal document costs.

When your dossier is complete, all of the notarized documents must be authenticated or apostilled. The correct state office will look at each notary signature, verify its authenticity, and then place an additional seal on the document. There is a per document cost of a few dollars, which adds up when you have a bunch of documents.

Finally, you will send your dossier to your agency, which, after reviewing, translates it into the corresponding language and forwards along to the adopting country. Be sure to mail your dossier via a service that provides detailed tracking.

Adoption Portfolio

If you are pursuing a domestic, newborn adoption, your adoption portfolio (sometimes called a *birth mother letter* or *family profile*) is perhaps the single most important thing you will do.

Twenty years ago, these profiles consisted of a simple "Dear Birth Parent" letter with a few photographs. Today, adoptive parents put together professional photo books to introduce their family to potential birth parents. Some also create custom websites and use social media—Twitter, Facebook, blogs, and Google ads to find a birth mother.

Imagine a birth mother sitting down with a stack of five or ten portfolios to look at and select the family she will choose to raise the child she is carrying. You want your portfolio to accurately reflect your family but also to stand out from the crowd.

Your adoption agency will give you its requirements. They may want to have your portfolio in multiple formats—hard copy, PDF, and so on. Some may ask for both a short version and a long version.

The first rule is *be genuine*! Of course you want to portray yourselves in the best possible light, but you also need to give the birth parents a real sense of who you are. For example, if you're a working mom, don't try to cover it up or gloss over it. Talk about why you love your work and the value it adds to your family.

You don't want to be an "OK" family for dozens of birth parents. You want to be the perfect family for *one*.

Pick photos and captions that tell a story. You want quality photographs that are close up and allow the birth families to see people's faces and their expressions. Be especially careful in choosing the photo for the front page. It is your first impression!

Let the captions for your photos go beyond stating the obvious. If you have a picture of yourselves in front of the Eiffel Tower, you could say "Joe and Sally visit the Eiffel Tower," but doesn't "We love to travel, see new things, and experience different cultures. We can't wait to share our sense of adventure with our child" sound much better?

Your agency will give you guidelines on what types of pictures to include. Know that it's OK to pose some shots. If playing board games is a big part of your family life but you don't have any photos to show it, ask a friend to come over and shoot some photos during your next game night.

"Show, don't tell" is a basic rule of writing that helps make your story compelling. "Sue works in an office" isn't quite as interesting as "As an executive assistant, Sue's organization and people skills help things run smoothly, a skill that will come in handy as a mom."

Again, there are companies that offer portfolio design services with costs ranging from $500 to $1,000. Many also offer complimentary design services for websites, business cards, and other networking materials. If the idea of writing your portfolio completely overwhelms you and you know you're not a great writer, it's worth it to ask for help.

Obtaining an Immigrant Visa

International adoptions require the added step of obtaining an immigrant visa before your child can enter the United States.

Once you have a completed your home study, submit form I-600A (Application for Advance Processing of Orphan Petition) and the corresponding fee to the U.S. Citizenship and Immigration Services. Once your I-600A is filed, you'll receive a request to appear at the local USCIS for fingerprinting…again. Anyone over the age of eighteen living in your household must be fingerprinted.

You want to do this as soon as you have your home study because the approval process can take several weeks or even months, and you must have an I-171H (the form you receive back from USCIS) as part of your dossier.

Adoption / Parenting Education

Once you've gotten through the initial burst of paperwork, you have time for education and training.

If you're adopting from foster care, you must complete state-required adoption classes. These classes may total between fifteen to thirty hours of education, spaced out over several weeks or months.

Adoption education for domestic, newborn adoptions will depend on agency and/or state requirements.

If you are adopting internationally from a Hague Convention country, you must complete ten hours of adoption education. If adopting from a non-Hague country, check to see if your agency requires a certain number of hours of training.

Even if you are not required to participate in training, I urge you not to skip this step. You may already have other children and feel confident in your parenting skills, but parenting an adopted child is different and requires new skills and tricks in your parenting toolbox. For example, the traditional "time out" can negatively affect an adopted child who is already feeling insecure about your love. Instead, adoption experts suggest a "time in" where the child remains close to you while you complete daily tasks or sits quietly next to you on the sofa for a few minutes.

A variety of training courses are available online. You may also receive credit for attending workshops at adoption and orphan care conferences. There are many books and resources, which you can find listed in the appendix to this book.

Referral Match

You've completed the paperwork and jumped through all the bureaucratic hoops. Now comes the hardest part—waiting. (You won't be twiddling your thumbs though. This is prime fund-raising time!)

During this time in foster care adoption, you and your caseworker work together to find the child or children who best fit your family and vice versa. Is your lifestyle compatible with the child's? Do you have the skills and knowledge to parent the child being considered? The child's personality, background, life experiences, medical, and emotional needs all come into play.

According to *Adoptive Families'* annual survey, 53 percent of those adopting from foster care received a placement that resulted in adoption within six months of finishing their certification.[1] Most agencies say to expect at least twelve months. Obviously, how open you are to age, gender, and race affects your wait time.

When a potential match is found, families receive information on the child and have an opportunity to ask additional questions. As things proceed, there is an opportunity to meet the child.

Remember, the professionals in charge of advocating for that child may consider multiple families, and their placement decision will be based on what is best for the child.

For domestic, newborn adoptions you might be surprised at how short the matching time can be. In the same *Adoptive Families* survey, 50 percent of parents were matched with a birth mother in six months or less from the time they completed their portfolio. Only 34 percent took longer than twelve months.

The waiting time for international adoptions varies greatly by country and even some by agency. China has the longest wait, by far, with 60 percent of traditional adoption referrals taking between three to five years. Parents adopting from Ethiopia generally receive a referral within eighteen to thirty-six months after dossier completion. South Korea completed 90 percent of referrals in fewer than eighteen months.

As mentioned in chapter 2, there is always some unpredictability when adopting from a foreign country. During our adoption in 2008, families adopting from Ethiopia were typically only waiting six to twelve months for a referral. But in the spring of 2011, Ethiopia's Ministry of Women, Children, and Youth Affairs decided to process a maximum of twenty adoption cases per day, a nearly 60 percent decrease. As a result, families sometimes wait up to three years to receive their referrals.

Ukraine adoption referrals are a bit unique in that you are required to travel to the country to be matched with your adoptive child. The local adoption authority gives the adoptive family information on children eligible for adoption. When you select a potential child, you receive a referral letter to go visit the child and obtain any medical and background information. You also meet and interact with the child. If the first child is not a suitable match, you can request a new referral. After three referrals, your adoption dossier is returned and additional paperwork must be completed in order to receive another referral.

International adoption referrals are matched based on the specifications set forth in your home study (age, race, medical needs) and usually in the order your dossier was submitted or logged in. Most agencies give you frequent updates on where you fall in the wait list. For example, they will say you are number twenty-seven for adoptions of ages infant to two. As families are matched, your number decreases. Adoptive parents tend to obsess over this number, eagerly awaiting the day when they get "the call."

When you are matched with a child your caseworker will call you with the good news, ready to e-mail you photos and information on the child. You might find yourself rushing to your spouse's place of employment or picking the kids up early from school so that you can all be together to "meet" the child for the first time. For fun, you might even want to videotape the moment.

Many parents describe the moment and say it was love at first sight, but it may not be that way for everyone. That's OK. You, and your spouse if you're married, will want to take time to carefully review the information you receive about the child to determine whether or not you are able to meet his or her needs.

You will receive photos, medical information (age, height, weight, lab tests for HIV, TB, hepatitis, any diagnosis and medications being taken), whatever background information is available (birth parent information, why the child is being placed, siblings if any), developmental information (milestones reached or missed such as rolling over, crawling, walking, and talking), and social information (how the child interacts with others).

You may choose to have the information reviewed by a doctor specializing in international adoption, especially if the referral information causes questions or concerns. These reviews range in cost from $100 to $300.

If you choose not to accept the referral, you are placed back at the top of the wait list. Be sure to communicate with your caseworker why you feel the match is not right, as it helps him or her make decisions regarding your next referral.

One alternative to choosing the traditional method of waiting for a referral is to consider a "waiting child." Most agencies have a list of children who have not yet been matched due to a variety of reasons. Age and medical needs are the biggest contributing factors to a child being on a wait list.

Medical needs could include something relatively minor such as a cleft palate—easily repairable in the United States—to severe developmental delays and major medical concerns that would change your day-to-day life.

My brother and his wife have completed three special needs adoptions from China. This shortened their adoptions to about a year versus the normal wait of three to five years for a healthy baby. Their children's special needs include a minor blood disorder and a child with a few missing fingers and repaired club feet. I might be biased, but they are three fantastic kids whose "special needs" require very little attention or lifestyle changes.

Adoptions of children with HIV are also on the rise as more families become educated and realize that with good medical care the life expectancy of someone with HIV is the same as a non-affected person. The truth is that HIV is spread three ways: sexual contact, IV drug use through the sharing of needles, and mother to infant (pregnancy, birth, or breast feeding). Because of this, HIV has never been transmitted in a normal family living environment. For more information on HIV adoption, visit ProjectHopeful.org.

Traveling / Becoming a Family

Most foster care adoptions happen within your own state, so the only traveling you will do is back and forth to classes and meetings.

Private, newborn adoptions may be done between birth parents and adoptive parents in two different states (called an interstate adoption), and so you may travel to the birth parents' state one or more times for an initial meeting and to pick up your new baby.

Travel is, of course, almost mandatory in the case of international adoption and is, in my opinion, one of the best parts of the process.

In some countries, you may be able to hire an escort to bring your child home instead of traveling yourself, at an additional cost. However, unless there is *no* other choice, I don't recommend this.

First, there is no better way to understand your adoptive child's culture and homeland than to experience it yourself. You will likely find yourself falling in love with the country. Both Mark and I have a deep love for Ethiopia, one that has led Mark to work full-time to promote orphan care in the country of our children's birth. To us, it feels like a second home.

Second, the process of leaving his or her homeland and everything he or she has ever known is going to be traumatic for your child. Why add to that stress by having him or her make that journey with a stranger, only to be thrust into the arms of a new group of strangers (you) when he or she arrives in the States?

Travel requirements vary by country. Some countries, including Ethiopia and Ukraine, require more than one trip although some parents choose to stay in country between the two required trips. This may save you some money but is not always feasible with work schedules and if there are other children in the home. The time period could be as short as four weeks or several months.

China, Colombia, South Korea, Vietnam, Taiwan, the Philippines, and Uganda only require one trip although in some cases that trip can be several weeks long.

Travel requirements, like any part of the adoption process, can change at any time. During our adoption in 2008, for example, Ethiopia adoptions only required one trip.

If you have other children in your family, it is up to you whether you decide to take them with you. You'll want to consider the added financial cost, how your children will do with the long airline ride, jet lag, strange foods, and the sometimes high stress. We chose not to take our two biological children due to the added expense and their young ages. We do, however, hope to take Wendemagegn and Beza back to Ethiopia someday, and Noah and Natalie will definitely accompany us then. I think it's important for them to see their siblings' birth country and experience their culture.

Your agency can tell you more about what to expect during travel. Most agencies send families in groups. You'll likely stay at a designated hotel and be driven around in a shuttle bus to appointments, meals, and visits with your child in a group with other adoptive families. Chances are you'll make some lifelong friends as you interact with your travel group.

Settling In at Home

Once you arrive home with your new child(ren), you'll need plenty of time to adjust to your new family life. Most experts advise families to take things slow and cocoon themselves for a while. Limit outside visitors and activities to allow you and your new child time to get to know each other and form healthy attachments.

You'll read and hear plenty on this subject during your education and training.

Finalizing the Adoption

At some point, you will complete the steps to finalize your adoption. With most domestic, newborn adoptions, this happens within six months. Foster care adoption finalization may take six to twelve months or more.

International adoption finalization requirements depend on several factors. It is best to ask your home study provider what your state requires. In Arizona, we were required to do what's called a "readoption" of Wendemagegn and Beza. Our social worker submitted a post-placement report (included in our initial home study fees), and we filed paperwork with the juvenile courts. There were no extra fees for us, and this process also gave us the opportunity to change the children's names if we wanted. (They got American middle names and the choice of which name to go by. Wendemagegn now goes by Luke.)

My husband and I appeared in front of a judge to answer a few questions, and our adoption was approved and finalized. Be sure to get at least two certified copies of your adoption decree before you leave court.

You'll also need to do things like obtain a social security card, birth certificate, and, in the case of international adoptions, a certificate of citizenship.

Connecting

If your child is from another country, make an effort to stay connected with his or her culture. Cook native foods, read books, watch movies, and talk often about his or her homeland. Adopted children frequently struggle with their identity as they grow up, and having a healthy racial/ethnic identity is crucial. A 2009 study by the Evan B. Donaldson Adoption Institute found that "a positive racial/ethnic identity is most effectively facilitated by 'lived' experiences such as travel to native country, attending racially diverse schools, and having role models of their own race/ethnicity."[2]

Parenting your adopted child is, of course, a lifelong process. Connect with other adoptive families, continue to read on the subject of parenting adopted kids, and, above all else, don't be afraid to ask for help if you need it.

CHAPTER FIVE
CONSIDERING THE COST

Chapter 2 gave some general financial information for the different types of adoptions, but let's break that down and go into more detail. What does the money pay for and how is it paid out? Luckily adoption fees are not all due at once.

Foster Care Adoption

As mentioned before, foster care adoption is the most affordable way to adopt. Many times there is absolutely no cost to the family, or there are reimbursements available to pay back expenses the adoptive family covers.

Costs you might incur include:

- Training Fees—Varies
- Home Study Fee—Up to $500
- Travel Fees (if the child is in a different state)—Varies

You can expect a foster care adoption to cost between nothing and $2,500.

Domestic Adoptions (Agency and Independent)

- Application Fee—$200–$750
- Home Study Fee—$1,500–$3,500
- Agency/Legal Fees—$15,000–$30,000
- Advertising/Networking—$750–$2,500
- Birth Mother Expenses—$5,000–$25,000

- Travel Expenses—Varies
- Out of Pocket—$150–$700

Application Fee—$200–$750

The application fee is simply the fee you pay when you first fill out your application to use the agency. It is often only a few hundred dollars and sent with the application that gets the ball rolling. Ask if this fee is refundable if you are not accepted by the agency.

Home Study Fee—$1,500–$3,500

The home study fee covers the cost of the written home study report that you will need for your state to approve you to adopt. You can expect to spend six to ten hours in conversation and meetings with your social worker. He or she then prepares the home study document that recommends you for adoption and gives specifics about the type of child you wish to adopt. It is quite an extensive document, around ten-plus pages. After your adoption is complete your home study provider is also required to do one or more post-placement reports. Fees for those may be included in the initial cost but be sure to ask for specifics.

Agency / Legal Fees—$15,000–$30,000

Agency and legal fees are the bulk of your adoption expense. This accounts for the actual services your adoption agency is going to provide to you and to the birth mother. It likely includes birth mother counseling, her general overhead expenses, costs to locate and terminate the birth father's rights, monitoring birth mother's medical updates, and completing all necessary paperwork before the child is born. Ask your agency if this fee is paid in one payment or if it can be spread out. Some agencies ask for a small amount when you are matched with a birth mother and require the balance when the child is born and placed for adoption. This safeguards you against losing a large chunk of money if the birth mother decides to parent her child.

Advertising /Networking—$750–$2,500

Advertising and networking fees may be paid directly to your agency or incurred privately if you are using an attorney and are primarily responsible for finding a birth mother. You will likely want to set up a separate phone number to use exclusively in your advertising. Printing expenses for business cards, photo books, or flyers should also be included.

Birth Mother Expenses—$5,000–$25,000

Birth mother expenses can vary greatly depending on your actual situation. In many cases the birth mother has medical insurance or is eligible for state Medicaid programs. If not, you cover her medical expenses including prenatal care, delivery, and postnatal care. That can add $10,000 or more to your adoption expenses. (Paying the birth mother expenses is optional and if presented with an unusually expensive situation you have the choice to decline and let her be matched with a different family.) Depending on state adoption laws, you may also be asked to cover basic living expenses such as rent, food, and transportation.

Some domestic adoptions do cross state borders and, if that is the case, be prepared for travel expenses. Unless it's close enough to drive, you will likely be purchasing last-minute, and therefore expensive, flights. Your stay in the birth mother's hometown could be anywhere from a couple of days to a week or more.

Out of Pocket—$150–$700

Out-of-pocket expenses are all the little things that are paid directly to a provider and can add up: getting copies of your marriage license and birth certificates for your home study, background clearance, local police clearance, medical exams, and so on.

With adoption there can always be unexpected expenses. A failed adoption may add $5,000 or more to your total costs. If you're doing an interstate adoption and the birth mother takes longer than anticipated to sign her termination papers, you may have a larger-than-expected travel total as you extend your stay. It is always a good idea to build in a buffer to prepare for these things.

International Adoption

Fees for international adoption can vary widely between agencies and depend on which country you plan to adopt from. But the good news is that they are usually set amounts with variance in only a couple of areas. The range below is given because of the variance from country to country. Once you decide where you are going to adopt from, the agencies you are looking at should provide you with an exact fee structure.

- Application Fee—$250–$750
- Home Study Fee—$2,500–$4,500
- Document Preparation and Authentication—$1,000–$2,000
- Agency and Program Fees—$10,000–$30,000 or more
- In-Country Adoption Expenses—$2,500–$12,000 or more
- Travel Expenses—$5,000–$15,000
- Out-of-Pocket Expenses—$1,000–$2,000
- Post-Adoption Expenses—$1,500–$2,500

Application Fee $250–$750

The application fee is simply what you pay when you complete your initial application with an agency. It may or may not be refundable if the agency does not accept you into the program.

Home Study Fee $2,500–$4,500

The home-study fee covers the same thing it does for a domestic adoption. The only difference is that if you are adopting from a Hague-accredited country there are additional home study requirements that may increase your expense.

Agency and Program Fees—$10,000–$30,000 or more

Agency and program fees are paid to your international adoption agency and cover the bulk of its services to you. What exactly is included should be clearly spelled out. Some agencies roll things like dossier translation and courier fees into their program fees. Others will list those items separately. Generally the fee includes helping you prepare your dossier, coordinating with immigration for the necessary paperwork, training costs, Hague compliance and, of course, the agency's general personnel, administrative, and overhead expenses. Program fees are often paid in multiple installments and at intervals such as program acceptance, referral, and travel.

In-Country Adoption Expenses—$2,500–$12,000 or more

In-country adoption expenses cover all the costs incurred in the other country. This includes governmental fees, overseas staff, in-country care of your child while in an orphanage or transition home, document translation, and certification. Again, this fee may be broken into installments by your agency.

Travel Expenses—$5,000–$15,000

Travel expenses of course vary widely based on a number of factors: (1) how many trips are required, (2) how many people travel, and (3) location. Even timing can affect your costs if your trips fall during peak season. In countries where multiple trips are required both parents may be required to come on at least one trip but follow-up trips can sometimes be taken by just one parent. If you choose to take any of your other children with you, this will of course add to the cost. Some agencies have a set travel package and require you to book travel through them. They have designated locations where families stay and take care of transportation, translators, and all the little details you might not want to worry about. Other countries and agencies give you total control over your travel plans, which can make it a little easier to save money. There are several organizations that specialize in helping adoptive families arrange flight and travel plans. I highly recommend contacting them for flights at a minimum. They have the knowledge required to book you the best deal with tickets that are easily changed in case you run into delays in-country. (See the appendix for a list of companies.)

Out-of-Pocket Expenses—$1,000–$2,000

Out-of-pocket expenses include all the little things you pay to someone other than your agency. And there are a lot of them. They include: fingerprint fees, medical reports, passport pictures, passports, travel immunizations, birth certificate copies, marriage license copy, medical exams, immigration fingerprint fee, immigration application I-600A. That last one is over $700 all by itself.

Post-Adoption Expenses—$1,500–$2,500

Post-adoption expenses include any post-placement reports you are required to complete, but there are additional expenses for internationally adopted children. You may be required to re-adopt the child depending on your adoption and the state you live in. That can cost a couple hundred dollars or over a thousand. You need to obtain a social security card (free) and then a new birth certificate. You will want certified copies of your final adoption decree. And finally, a Certificate of Citizenship for your newly adopted child costs $550.

While international adoption expenses are generally very specific and known, this area also has perhaps the biggest potential for unknown expenses. Generally that happens if there are major changes in the adoption laws of the country you are adopting from or the time to referral takes longer than expected.

As mentioned in chapter 2, international adoption can be unpredictable. If a country suddenly closes its doors to adoption, you are left with the choice of stopping or choosing to switch to a different country. In the case of the latter you will often have already paid fees that will never be recouped. This can add thousands of dollars to your total cost. Or perhaps the initial wait time you were given suddenly changes because the country implemented new guidelines and rules. Several of the documents that you prepare as part of your dossier, such as your home study, fingerprints, and I-600, are only good for a certain amount of time. If that time lapses before your adoption is complete, you pay additional costs to renew or redo paperwork. Some adoptive families have had to renew paperwork multiple times before their child is finally brought home.

While rare, there have also been cases of families who hit snags once they were in-country to pick up their child that resulted in weeks, even months, of additional time in-country.

So it is always a good idea to build a little padding into your budget. I would factor in between $3,000 to $5,000.

Of course raising a child costs money and your normal household budget will need to be adjusted for things like a bigger grocery budget and larger clothing allowance. Depending on the age of the child you adopt, consider what things you might need right away and add that to your adoption budget. This might include clothes, diapers, car seat, and a stroller. Or in the case of an older child you might want to have a bike or a scooter and some sports equipment. Will you need a larger vehicle?

However, these types of things should not be included in the costs you are fund-raising. This is just so that you are prepared.

It is also likely that you will have some medical expenses the first few months as you catch up with immunizations and do eye and dental checkups.

Budgeting Your Adoption

After you've selected your agency or attorney you should have a solid idea of what you can expect to pay for your adoption. While exact timelines are impossible to predict, do your best to guess when the different fees will be due. This will help you plan, budget, and know when to start the process.

Of course the ideal situation is that you bought this book a year or two before you plan on starting the adoption process. If that's you then you're in an ideal spot to start saving and planning for your adoption. The best thing you can do is get a good handle on your household finances and find ways to trim expenses and put away money. Chapter 8 goes into more detail on how to do this.

However, I'm guessing that the majority of you are either just months away from starting the process or have already waded into the adoption waters. Once God places adoption on your hearts it beats to a different drummer. And sometimes we let that drummer get out of control. It's easy to get caught up in the emotions and the excitement and jump in with all the enthusiasm of a two-year-old in a candy store.

Once Mark and I had the initial conversation about adoption, things moved pretty fast. Two months later we were filling out the application and starting the "paper chase" to bring Wendemagegn and Beza home. I was, as I'm guessing most moms are, fully emotionally invested in those kids within a matter of days after we saw their video. They were mine and every day without them was torturous and unacceptable. OK, yes, I'm being a tad melodramatic but honestly, that's what happens to parents.

I wouldn't change anything about our story because I know without a shadow of a doubt that God meant Wendemagegn and Beza for our family. But if I could give you a piece of advice I would say this—take a deep breath.

Now take another one.

God knows. He knows your heart's desire. He knows the road that has brought you to this point whether it is through the pain of infertility or through a desire to be the family for a child who has none. And He knows your child. He knows where he or she is right this moment or the exact moment he or she will be born.

Rest in His timing. Spend time in prayer both alone and with your spouse as you gather information, talk through options, do your research, and talk with other adoptive families.

I think international adoption can be extra emotionally charged. During your research you've read overwhelming statistics, seen pictures of kids in horrible conditions, and read amazing adoption stories. It's easy to work ourselves into a frantic pace, spurred by the thought that we must rescue these kids and do it as soon as possible. After all, it sometimes is quite literally a matter of life and death. But, if you let that fear set the tone for your adoption, it will only lead to anxiety and at least one bout of full-on ugly crying when you come face-to-face with the reality that you are powerless against paperwork delays and foreign governments.

God holds adoption in His hands. Of course this is much easier for me to say, being on this side of the adoption process, but God so clearly orchestrated the timing of our adoption that it serves as a constant reminder to me that He is in control and that is a good thing. For someone who is a "control enthusiast," that is a hard thing to let go.

In short, don't let fear and anxiety push you into making unwise decisions.

Use this sheet as a guide to help plan for and track expenses. You can download an Excel version on my website at juliegumm.com/book-extras/. There are also several planning documents included in the Adoption Finance Toolkit on Resources4Adoption.com.

Table 1: Domestic

	Estimated Cost Range ($US)	Actual Cost	Date Due
Home study	1,000–2,500		
Certified birth & marriage certificates	100–300		
Criminal record checks	25–100		
Postage	200		
Notarization / authentication of documents	500-1,000		
Application fee	100-500		
Attorney / agency fees	12,000-25,000		
Advertising / networking	500-2,000		
Birthparent expenses	5,000-20,000		
Travel / meals / lodging (if applicable, per person, round-trip)	1,500-2,500		
Post-placement report	500-1,500		
Certified court documents	50		
Certificate of citizenship	600		

Table 2: International

	Estimated Cost Range ($US)	Actual Cost	Date Due
Home study	2,000–3,500		
Certified birth & marriage certificates	100–300		
Criminal record checks	25–100		
Postage	200		
Notarization / authentication of documents	500-1,000		
USCIS I-600A	720		
Travel vaccinations	150-500		
Passports (per person)	125		
Visas (per person)	20-150		
Dossier authentication	100-200		
Agency application fee	100-500		
Agency fee	8,000-12,000		
Foreign agency fees	2.500-12,000		
Orphanage donation	500-3,000		
Child's medical exam	50-200		
Child's passport / visa	300-500		
Airfare (per person, round-trip)	1,500-2,500		
Meals	500-750		
Lodging	500-1,000		
Interpreter	250-500		
Excursions / souvenirs	250-500		
Post-placement report	500-1,000		
Re-adoption fee	100-500		
Birth certificate	25		
Certified court documents	50		
Certificate of citizenship	600		

CHAPTER SIX
THE DEBT-FREE APPROACH

Mark and I estimated that by the time we were home with the kids, our adoption would cost us between $25,000 to $30,000. Yikes!

We had been paying about $2,200 a month toward our house payment for the previous two and a half years. With it paid off, we knew we had that money to use. At the time, we were told that we could complete the adoption in six months. (That makes me laugh now.) That would allow us to have $13,200. We had our $10,000 "emergency fund" and were willing to put that money toward the costs. But we would still be a bit short.

I knew there were grants available, but was afraid we wouldn't qualify because of our income and being debt-free. I also knew there were several avenues to obtaining interest-free adoption loans.

Mark and I discussed this one night. Or rather, I said something like, "Well, I guess if we have to do an interest-free loan, we will; then we'll just pay it off as quickly as we can."

Mark gave me an unenthusiastic "uh huh."

Neither of us was completely enthralled with that idea. We committed eight years earlier to never go into debt again. We had just gotten debt-free. We weren't arguing that this wasn't a worthy cause, but we didn't feel much peace about it. Taking on a loan felt too much like going back on a promise.

Several weeks later, I visited my best friend. One night while flipping television channels, I found Dave Ramsey's show on the Fox Business Channel. Since I hadn't seen the show, I stopped to see what it was like. The program was a call-in format, very similar to his radio program.

About five minutes later, a man called and explained he really felt God calling him to a career change, which meant going to chiropractic school and incurring quite a bit of student loan debt. Dave Ramsey encouraged the man to find creative ways to finance his schooling or wait and save up the money. I wasn't surprised.

Then Dave uttered the words that rocked my world.

"There is not one example in the Bible of God calling someone to do something and then using debt as a tool to accomplish it."

Ouch! I felt like I'd been hit with a sledge hammer. I had such little faith. Sure, I knew God could provide the means for us to adopt. But here I was, trying to take control and figure out *how* He would provide. I had put God in an itty-bitty box and forgotten how powerful He truly is.

God knew about our commitment to live debt-free. So why would He ask us to adopt and then make debt part of our process?

When I told Mark what I heard, he said, "Well, I've been thinking the same thing, but I was afraid you'd be upset if I told you." He was probably right. But from that point on, we committed to adopting without going into debt.

A month later career changes made this challenge seem even more daunting. Mark left his full-time job. It was a decision that had been examined from every angle and prayed through endlessly—something we knew God was asking him to do. Of course we prayed that God would follow quickly with Mark's "next thing," but circumstances weren't that easy. Mark ended up being unemployed throughout our adoption.

Six months earlier, I had returned to work part-time as a graphic designer for our church. A few weeks before Mark resigned, I was offered a full-time position as communications director. So as Mark stepped away, I stepped into a full-time role that provided benefits and a salary. But the salary was less than half of what Mark had earned. That "extra" $2,200 a month we had hoped to have without a house payment was gone. We could pay the bills and save a couple hundred dollars each month, but suddenly our adoption costs presented a whole new set of obstacles.

We were incredibly grateful to even be in the position where Mark could leave his job. If we had not been debt-free, his job shift would have been so much harder.

Our debt-free adoption commitment was going to take God-sized miracles. Yet we remained steadfast in our determination. We did not want to give up the freedom we had found in being debt-free and we did not want to keep God from teaching us to rely more fully on Him as the Great Provider.

CHAPTER SEVEN
ADOPTION DEBT: WRONG OR RIGHT?

Is it a sin to go into debt for an adoption?

Simple answer? No.

In fact, scripture never says that debt is sinful. There are, however, numerous scriptures that warn against debt.

But, let's be honest. Why are people usually in debt? Other than a home mortgage and perhaps medical bills, most debt is the result of wanting something we cannot afford. Or not having the self-discipline to save up for what we want. We don't have $30,000 for that shiny new SUV? Put it on a six-year payment plan. Those new shoes are too cute to pass up? Lay down the plastic.

It's materialism, plain and simple.

Our culture has created an "I deserve it" attitude that gets worse with each generation. I grew up driving the family cars—paid-for vehicles, one that reached the vintage age of seventeen before my brother totaled it. Yet six months into our marriage Mark and I were signing papers for a $10,000 car loan—while we were both students and had a monthly income of $450! When we graduated we added a second car and a second loan. Everyone has car payments, right? Why live in a two-bedroom apartment when we could get a no-money-down mortgage?

Scripture's warnings about debt come from the knowledge that when we are in debt, it often means our priorities are out of whack.

Matthew 6:24 says, "No one can serve two masters. Either you will hate the one and love the other, or you will be devoted to the one and despise the other. You cannot serve both God and money" (NIV).

The issue is not the debt; it is what the debt represents. It represents our priorities, our heart, and our "master." If my priority is driving nice cars, having the latest fashions, and having the nicest house of all my friends, then I have fallen into sin. If I am discontent with what God has provided for me to live on, and feel the need to better my lifestyle via Visa, then I have fallen into sin.

However, no one is going to claim that the root of adoption is materialism. Bringing a child into your family is usually motivated by the complete opposite—love, selflessness, and obedience to God's call to care for the orphan.

I know families who have sold their cars and furniture, emptied out 401(k)s and downsized their homes and they still came up short when the adoption bill was due. What do you do when it's time to board the plane and you have no other options? Would I tell you to give up and forget the adoption? Of course not.

But more often, I think debt becomes the answer when we don't want to be uncomfortable, when we aren't willing to put in the extra work it would take to be debt-free. Figuring out how to get out of a car lease or get by on one car means time, energy, and sacrifice. Getting up at 5:00 a.m. to pick up a newspaper route is no one's idea of fun. Spend countless hours organizing fund-raisers or relax in front of the television after a long day: which one sounds more comfortable?

Selling your $20,000 car and replacing it with a modest $5,000 vehicle may seem like a long-term sacrifice for a short-term need. But if my experience is any indication, by the time you bring your child home, you won't even miss it.

Even when for a good cause, debt is still a hardship. The future is unknown and that Christmas bonus you think will zero out your adoption loan balance may not happen. Even relying on the adoption tax credit is not a sure thing. What happens if you come home and your new child has an unexpected medical issue that racks up $10,000 in medical bills?

I've seen firsthand the stress debt causes in a marriage and that is not my wish for anyone. Your marriage is going to need every ounce of reserve strength it has to get through the first few months home. You do not need to be stressing over loan payments.

If it comes down to it and you end up needing a loan, do not take out a home equity loan, line of credit, or put it on your Visa! There are several interest-free adoption loan programs available including ABBA Fund and Lifesong for Orphans.

Trust God. Trust in His timing. Trust that He is watching over your child while you work to bring him or her home. Trust in His provision.

Adopting without going into debt is possible. This book gives you the tools and it can be done. It will take work and it will take sacrifice, but it is possible.

CHAPTER EIGHT
IT STARTS WITH SACRIFICE

When faced with a large obstacle, like an expensive adoption bill, taking the first step is the hardest.

Where do you start?

The best place is with the money you already have.

The word *budget* can be a scary and depressing word. Trust me; I felt the same way for the first six years of our marriage. Our budget never seemed to work for very long and overwhelmed me.

But as Mark and I learned from experience, if you don't have a budget, you are "leaking" money; money that can go toward your adoption.

So stop thinking of a budget as a restrictive, fun-killing necessity. Instead, think of it as a simple plan that tells your money where to go. Would you rather manage your money or have your money (or lack thereof) manage you?

Grab a notepad, your checkbook, your computer (if you bank online), and your spouse. Sit down and list all your fixed monthly expenses—mortgage, car payments, gas, utilities, cell phones, internet, debt payments, and so on. Next, estimate how much you spend for things like groceries, clothing, entertainment, eating out, gifts, and miscellaneous expenditures. Add it up. Compare it to your monthly income. Income minus expenses should equal $0. If you're in the positive (and have leftover money), congratulations. Take that dollar figure and assign it to "adoption savings."

If you're in the negative, well, we have a problem already don't we? No time like the present to fix it. The next section explains some of the top ways to save money and help your bottom line. Hopefully by implementing these you'll be able to get into the positive and start putting away money for your adoption.

Early on (pre-Dave Ramsey), we mistakenly tried to create a generic monthly budget that worked all the time. But life isn't the same from month to month, is it? One month it's back-to-school shopping, the next it's birthday parties. Each month is unique and so your spending plan must flex accordingly.

If you prefer spreadsheets that will do the calculations for you, use your computer. It's the easiest method for me, and it's helpful to look back on previous months and compare budgets. A few days before pay day I take out the budget and my calendar and go through each category to see what needs to be adjusted.

But really, I'm not the best one to teach you about budgets; you need Dave Ramsey's book *Total Money Makeover*. The book covers not only budgeting but also eliminating debt, saving, investing, and more. I also highly recommend Financial Peace University (FPU), a nine-week class that expands on the book material in an environment that provides personal support and encouragement. (Or you can purchase the home study FPU kit.)

If this is your first time to use a budget, know that it will take you a couple months to fine tune it. Many people have no idea how much money to budget for things like groceries and clothing. Save all your receipts during these months; this will help you see what you're spending.

Once you've developed a budget, the key is to stick to it. Over the years, we found the best way for us to stick to our budget is to use cash. After I pay the regular bills (utilities, cell phone, insurance, mortgage, and so on), I determine our budgeted amounts for items like groceries, entertainment, eating out, clothes, and medicine. I withdraw that amount of cash on payday and put it in envelopes clearly labeled for each category.

When the money is gone, it's gone. When the kids pester you to order delivery pizza, you can look in your Eating Out envelope and see whether you can afford it. The only exception to this rule is our gas money, which gets left in the checking account so I can use the debit card to pay at the pump.

Studies show that people spend 12 to 18 percent less when they use cash instead of plastic (even debit cards). So we try *really* hard to use the debit card only for fuel. We're certainly not perfect, but I can tell you that on the months when we "fall off the wagon" we blow our budget every time.

It takes a little getting used to and some time to figure out what envelopes work best for you. When we first started I had an envelope for groceries, one for toiletries, and one for household stuff. Standing in the checkout aisle at Walmart trying to estimate how much came out of each envelope was such a pain that I quickly decided one envelope for those categories worked just as well.

If you're not comfortable carrying around that much cash, try withdrawing the whole amount on payday but only putting half of it in the envelopes. At the end of a week, put the other half in.

And yes, borrowing from another envelope is allowed.

Besides the monthly reviews of our budget, each time our family income changes (up or down), we reassess and adjust accordingly. On the one hand, living on a pretty lean budget was nice. On the other hand, this meant we couldn't squeeze out a lot of extra money for our adoption when Mark left his job.

Our family still found ways to save money by cutting back more on entertainment and eating out. I also knew I'd had my last pedicure, a rare treat anyway, for a *long* time. Whenever I felt tempted to pick up some new item of clothing or DVD, those two beautiful faces would flash before my eyes and the item would go back on the shelf. Every penny counted.

Once you've established your household budget, take a long hard look to see where you can cut expenses and find more money for your adoption.

From our own personal experience and from working with dozens of couples while teaching Financial Peace University through our church, the following areas seem to be the top categories to trim and reap the most reward.

Eating Out

The average American household spends nearly $220 a month eating away from home.[1] Brown bagging your lunch might not be as much fun as eating out with your coworkers, but the savings add up quickly. Pack leftovers from last night's dinner or take a frozen entree instead. Budget to eat lunch out maybe once a week or every other week instead of every day. The added bonus is that you can use your lunch hour to catch up on reading all those adoption parenting books.

Look at how often your family eats out and when. If your family is like mine, eating out was occasionally planned, but, more often than not, it was a last resort. As in "I can't think what to make for dinner" or "I'm too tired to make something" or "everyone is starving and when we get home I have no idea what I'll fix."

Now I make sure that we always have a couple of frozen pizzas in the freezer, as well as some of those easy family skillet meals. I don't suggest making those the majority of your grocery list because that's expensive too. But if a $7 pasta meal will save you from a $45 restaurant bill, it's worth it. My kids also love when I make breakfast for dinner—eggs and pancakes are always a hit and I always have the ingredients on hand.

Now as a busy mom of four, the Crock-Pot is my favorite kitchen appliance. When I'm doing my meal planning I look at our calendar and try to plan Crock-Pot meals for those days when we have kids sports games or I'm going to be gone all day at an event. It's nice knowing we'll come home to a hot meal with minimal work and it saves the temptation to grab fast food for everyone on the way home.

I've also been known to declare "fend for yourself" night and everyone just eats whatever they want—leftovers, cereal, or PB&J. Seriously, no one is going to need therapy if there isn't a three-course meal every night for dinner.

Before we started the adoption process, we had already cut down on our eating out. We usually took the kids to the local pizza and game place about once a month ($30) and then maybe two or three fast food stops each month. That still added up to about $100 a month.

We cut our pizza nights to once every other month and had more family movie nights at home with a rented DVD and frozen pizza, or "make your own pizza" night. The kids loved it just as much. Our budget loved it more.

I also kept a bag of snacks in the car to help stave off the hunger that often drove us to the fast food places in desperation. On the occasions when we went through a drive-thru, we learned to eat off the value menu, drink water and, to the despair of my kids, we stopped ordering the kids meal. (You know you just throw away the toy two weeks later when they're not looking!)

Possible Monthly Savings: $100–$200

Groceries

The U.S. Department of Labor estimates that the average American family of four spends roughly $600 a month on groceries.[2] How do you compare?

What if I told you that you could feed that same family of four on $75 a week—half the national average? That's $200 a month for adoption expenses.

Now that we have four kids at home, I spend about $100 to $125 a week on groceries. (When I say "groceries," I am also including cleaning supplies, paper goods, and basic toiletries.) Mary Ostyn, author of *Family Feasts for $75 a Week* and an adoptive mom, has seven kids living at home and feeds their family for approximately $800 a month. (Her book is a great resource to learn more about saving on groceries. Plus it has wonderful recipes.)

So, how do I do it? I'll give you the basics. It comes down to three things: planning, weekly sales, and coupons.

Planning

The key to sticking to a grocery budget (and avoiding the nothing-to-eat-so-we'll-go-out quandary) is a menu plan. A day or two before payday, I prepare a meal plan for that pay period. I include main dishes, side items, and a dessert if needed (which is not very often—another way to save). I make my menu with my calendar open so I can see what nights we will be gone, what nights dad will be gone (which means I make something really easy like grilled cheese sandwiches), and what days we have after-school activities and limited meal prep time.

One thing I love about the recipes in *Family Feasts for $75 a Week* is that they don't require twenty different ingredients, half of which are not pantry staples and require more of your grocery budget. The meals I make often are pretty simple and don't require expensive, fancy groceries. I satisfy my foodie tendencies on the occasional out-of-town vacation where I like to visit a nice restaurant one night and try some fancy new dish.

After planning my menu, I check my pantry to see if I have the ingredients for each meal. I add anything I am missing to my grocery list. My goal is to make two large shopping trips each month and no more than two quick trips for things like milk and fresh produce. Because I'm a Type-A personality, I actually developed a printable grocery list template that follows the layout of my local Walmart. I have a section for each aisle where I list my needs. It saves me from being almost done and realizing I forgot something way at the back of the store. My husband still teases me about this list.

I've invested a bit of time to create a list of "standard" meals that I make for our family for easy reference. As I try new recipes and find successful ones, I add them to the list. If you can find thirty to forty meals your family likes, put them on an easy rotation system.

Several companies exist that will help you with your meal planning. Emeals (emeals.com) is a subscription service that, for $5 per month, provides weekly meal plans based on grocery store sales for a variety of stores. The weekly menus include recipes, instructions, and a grocery shopping list that has an average weekly cost of $75. They provide plans for special diets like gluten-free and low carb, too.

If you're tech driven and Mac-based, one of my all time favorite apps is called Paprika. It's a recipe management, meal planning, and grocery list tool all in one. You can save recipes you find online into the app with one click, assign it to a meal plan calendar date, and it will automatically create a grocery list for you. It also allows you to easily multiply servings.

Weekly Sales

Your local grocery store most likely has weekly sales. Ours seem to cycle on a Wednesday-through-Tuesday pattern, and the new ads arrive in the Wednesday paper or in the mail. If you don't get copies of your store circulars delivered, you can find them online.

As I'm menu planning, I look at what's on sale, particularly in the meat department. If chicken is on sale, it's very likely we'll be eating lots of chicken-based dishes. I also watch the fruit and produce deals. Over time, I have come up with my "maximum spend" list. For example, I will not pay more than $1 per pound for apples. If I can't buy them for that or less, then I don't buy any. (Frequently, they are as cheap as 33 cents a pound.) We eat apples and bananas pretty much year-round and then add whatever fruit is seasonal and on sale.

I have the luxury of a chest freezer in the garage, which has proved invaluable. (Our first one was purchased used for $150 and lasted us seven years. About the time it was on its last legs my parents gave us theirs when they upgraded.) When meat or poultry goes on sale for a really great price (like boneless, skinless chicken breasts for $1.57 per pound), I stock up. Depending on my grocery budget that month, I might buy four packages, or I might buy eight.

Then in my next menu planning cycle, I know I have chicken, and I add some chicken dishes to the menu. That saves me money on that week's groceries that I can use to stock up on another item on sale at a really good price.

Now, if you're like me, when someone mentions shopping multiple stores to take advantage of all the sales, your eyes glaze over. Because, you know, I have all that spare time—*not*.

But did you know that Walmart will match their competitor's prices? That means if apples are on sale for 34 cents a pound at one store, milk for $1.49 at another and you're going to Walmart for other items, you only need to make *one* trip. Take the competitor's ads with you and when the cashier gets to the sale item just say "That is price matched at $1.49." Sometimes they ask to see the ad, but most cashiers familiarize themselves with the weekly ads. I've even had a couple of cashiers tell me a better price than the one I knew about. They won't match "buy one, get one free" or percent off offers. Also the meat has to be packaged the same way as the other store. For example if Kroger's prepackaged three-pound tube of hamburger is $.99 a pound you can't get the in-store butchered Walmart hamburger for the same price. You have to buy a prepackaged tube.

To help the cashier, and myself, I try to group all my price-matched items in one area of the shopping cart and then load them on the belt at the end of my order. The people in line behind you will thank you too.

Coupons

When it comes to coupons there tend to be three groups of people—those that hate them, those that use them occasionally, and the fanatics (and I mean that lovingly). Goodness, there are even reality television shows now like *Extreme Couponing*. Relax, I'm not asking you to spend thirty hours a week clipping and organizing coupons.

There are tons of websites, blogs, and subscription services that will show you how to save *hundreds* of dollars on groceries every month. I've included some great websites in the appendix.

Before our adoption, I would have put myself in the second category. I'd clip coupons sometimes, and save a few bucks here and there. But for the most part, I didn't bother. A lot of the coupons were for name brands and I felt like store brands saved us just as much money with less work.

My husband, however, *loves* a good bargain, especially the hunt for the bargain. Apparently, he had too much time on his hands during ten months of unemployment. He stumbled upon one of the websites that explained how to save tons of money at Walgreens and CVS. Next thing I knew, our linen closet had enough shampoo, conditioner, body wash, razors, deodorant, toothpaste, toothbrushes, cough syrup, facial wash, and air freshener to last us five years. I'm not exaggerating; we are still living off of it. In all, I would say that he spent around $50 to $75 for what is easily $400 to $500 worth of toiletries.

Granted, he spent a lot of time pursuing those bargains, but he had fun and it helped contribute to our adoption fund by freeing up money.

But Mark was reluctant to tackle grocery couponing since grocery shopping was my domain. He sent me a few links to coupon sites, though, and educated me on the lingo.

After the kids came home and I was now feeding six mouths, I became motivated to learn how to become a better coupon user. What I discovered was that by combining coupons, weekly sales, and store coupon policies (like doubling, tripling, and so on) it was possible to get $175 in groceries for $30. Yes, I said $30. Now that $30 worth of groceries won't necessarily go together to make a meal. But, by stockpiling sale items you save money in future months. I've been known to come home with twenty boxes of cereal when I can get it for 49 cents a box.

The caveat is that more advanced couponing *will* require trips to multiple stores. The reason advanced coupling works so well is combining store specials with their double/triple coupon policies. But using the websites listed in the appendix will save you a ton of time. I'd say that I never spent more than a couple hours a week scanning the lists, finding the coupons, and stopping at the appropriate store—

often on my lunch break. Most of the items tend to be dry goods so keeping them cold wasn't an issue.

I know a lot of people who talk about saving money on groceries and household items mention buying in bulk at warehouse stores. But if you're not careful, you can walk out having spent your weekly grocery money and not be able to make a single meal out of what's in your grocery cart.

I've learned that just because it's in bulk doesn't necessarily mean it's cheaper—especially when you take into consideration discounts after coupons. We have a few grocery items that I regularly buy at warehouse stores but everything else I buy at regular stores on sale or with coupons. I feel like it is easier for me to stick to my monthly budget this way.

Possible Monthly Savings: $200

Entertainment and Media Services

When we started our adoption, we downgraded our satellite TV package and saved about $30 a month. About four years ago (long after the kids were home), we realized we hardly watched anything on the satellite channels. We had already limited our kids' TV watching to the weekends, Mark rarely watches anything other than sports, and most of my favorite shows are on network television.

Quite honestly, the thing I loved most about our satellite service was the digital video recorder. Now, thanks to the wonders of network and subscription websites, you can watch most TV shows online at your convenience.

Our $8 per month Netflix subscription lets us stream shows through our Wii. Netflix has a ton of TV episodes, Disney Channel movies, and family movies for the kids, and they've even discovered some of the old favorites like *The Cosby Show*. For those with Amazon Prime accounts you also have access to their streaming library.

You might want to check out the Roku device. This allows you to stream Netflix, Amazon on Demand, and many other media channels that can help replace that paid satellite or cable service. We bought a used Roku device for about $50.

Our family also learned to wait for movies to come out on video. Or we look for theaters that offer "first matinee showing" tickets at $5. Check your library for free videos or find a Redbox near you and rent them for $1.50 a night.

The average family spends over $200 a month on entertainment. In the course of twelve to eighteen months that could be almost $3,000 toward your adoption.

It's hard, if not impossible, to imagine living without cell phones. But you can shop around and see if you can find a cheaper plan, possibly combining phones into a family program.

Four years ago our cell phone contract expired and we purposefully refrained from extending it. I admit, the allure of a free new phone is tempting. But instead, we've purchased new-to-us phones on eBay and maintained our flexibility. There are several services such as Walmart Family Mobile, Straight Talk, Cricket, Boost, and Virgin mobile that offer unlimited talk and text plans for about $45 to $50 per phone. The move saved us $100 a month. Also, even now at ages eleven to fourteen our kids don't have cell phones. We haven't found it necessary but when it is, we will probably opt for a pay-as-you-go phone that can be handed to whatever child needs it when they go to a friend's house.

A lot of families have already eliminated their home phone and just use their cell phones. I never wanted to do that when our kids were younger in case they needed to call 9-1-1. We talked about it again, but didn't want their friends calling our cell phones, which are also our primary work phones.

With a little research, Mark found the perfect solution. Ooma is a voice over IP service, similar to Vonage, but without the monthly fee. We bought a refurbished Ooma Hub box for $99. It plugs into our wireless internet router and then into our existing phone handset base. We still have caller ID, call waiting, and voice mail, but we only pay taxes and government fees each month. Instead of $25 a month, we're spending $4. The box pays for itself in five months and then we get to enjoy the savings.

Possible Monthly Savings: $300 or more

Gifts

Gift-giving can grow ridiculously expensive between family, friends, and kids. Years ago, we decided, jointly with our families, to adjust the system.

Christmas: Each year, the adults draw names so they buy for one other adult. Typically, we spend about $40 to $50 for that gift. Then we buy for all the nieces and nephews. For us that's eleven kids, but giving gifts to kids is way more fun than adults anyway. We spend about $10 to $15 for each child and have occasionally pooled this money for one family to purchase a group gift they can all enjoy—like a new Wii game. We spend a little bit more on our own kids, but we still don't go overboard—around $40 per child.

If the kids have a more expensive item on their Christmas list, then we'll often go in with my parents or one of the aunts and uncles to purchase the gift. Our kids know that the more expensive their wish list, the fewer gifts they'll receive.

Some of you may spend even less, but for some others $40 may seem like a drastic cut. You might even have teenage children who would stage a revolt. Odds are, especially if you're pursuing international adoption, your money values are beginning to shift as you realize the incredible wealth we have as Americans when compared to the rest of the world. I think we have a responsibility to teach our children how fortunate they are.

Birthdays: My husband and I don't buy birthday gifts for our siblings anymore. Instead, we just send a heartfelt note. We still buy for our parents, because well, they deserve it! We buy for nieces and nephews, again spending $10 to $15 each. (With eleven kids, it still adds up.) Because all of our nieces and nephews are out of state (and two are out of the country), we often just send cash that they can go shopping with.

I have a couple of close friends who I like to celebrate birthdays with because they mean a lot to me. But usually that means taking them out to dinner and enjoying a night together (at least for those who live locally). We don't do gifts on top of that.

With four kids, it seems like someone is always coming home from school with a birthday party invitation. My daughter had five parties within the first six weeks of school one year. We finally realized we had to tell them that we might not go to all the parties. Obviously, they attend the birthday parties of their really close friends, but I can usually gauge how close they are by how much our kids talk about that child on a normal basis. Thankfully, it seems that as the kids get older there are fewer parties where every single kid in the class is invited.

Again, our spending limit is about $10 to $15. As I'm out shopping, I always keep an eye out for clearance toys and great prices on appropriate gifts. I buy them and put them away in a box in my closet. When we get a party invitation, we check the box before we make a trip to the store. I confess that I like this method mostly because it saves me from spending thirty minutes in the toy aisle while my child decides what to get the birthday kid. Torturous!

I've had to absolve myself of some initial feelings of guilt because we don't spend as much on gifts as other families. But I realized most of that was self-imposed and out of some silly need to impress other parents. The birthday child certainly doesn't care as long as the gift is thoughtful and something he or she will enjoy.

Speaking of birthday parties, we also scaled back on how we celebrate our children's birthdays. It's easy to get caught up in all the event birthday parties, but you can easily spend $300 to $400 on a birthday celebration. Instead, on their birthday, they can invite two friends for a sleepover. Sometimes we'll go to Peter Piper Pizza, but most of the time we just make them a special birthday dinner, rent a movie, and let them hang out, play video games, and have fun with their friends. It's a lot less stress on me, and the kids enjoy it just as much. Yes, it means I have a mess to clean up at home afterward but everyone pitches in and we make short work of it. We'll do something special for the major milestones, like thirteen and sixteen. As they get older I imagine the number of invited friends will increase in proportion with their maturity level.

Possible Monthly Savings: $25–$100

The Impulse Buy

I found that I saved a lot of money during our adoption process by just resisting the small impulse purchases—the cute $10 shirt, the newest Disney movie on DVD, the Starbucks drink, and so on.

Honestly, we buy so much unnecessary stuff. For me it was mostly clothes. It doesn't seem that big a deal to pick up a $10 shirt here or a cute pair of shoes for $15. But it adds up.

Two years after the kids were home I was having a "we have too much stuff" meltdown as I put away the kids' winter clothes and got out their summer wear. I realized that they *never* wore half the clothes I was putting away. I had them all come down to the living room where it looked like a shopping mall had exploded. I told them to pick out ten outfits—ten shirts, ten pants, and a few dresses for the girls. We do laundry once a week so that was plenty. This allowed them to pick out their favorite stuff and then I gave the rest away.

Now when my husband heard what I was doing he said, "I'm up for the ten item challenge, are you?"

A part of me wanted to do a little happy dance. I like to tease Mark that he has more clothes than I do. And he does. At one point I counted his polo shirts and he had eighty-seven of them. Now, he had gotten every single one of them as either a gift or purchased at the thrift store so there wasn't a lot of money invested. But it was the excess that bothered me, the fact that he really only wore about the same fifteen shirts over and over. (See, my Type-A personality coming out again.)

On the other hand, I spend more on my clothes (I am still a bargain shopper) but I regularly purge out items that don't fit, are out of style, or I just don't wear. Of course, I too have way more than I need.

We ended up having a really good conversation about excess versus money spent and before I knew it, Mark had challenged me to go twelve months without shopping for myself—clothes, shoes, purses, accessories, and so on.

Now, if there's one way to get me to do something, it's to imply that you don't think I can. I'm stubborn this way. Mark and I are also a little competitive. So, man, he was *on*! Challenge accepted. He agreed to do it too.

For the most part, abstaining from shopping wasn't as hard as I expected. It did make me realize how often I would pick up something little here and there.

During those twelve months I stayed away from the mall and avoided the unnecessary sections of Walmart and Target that only tempted me and made me dissatisfied with what I had. I also found it helpful to avoid the fashion magazines, catalogs, and online stores. Contentment is a lot easier when you're not comparing what you have to what everyone else has.

If Mark had issued the no-shopping challenge during our adoption journey, I'm sure we could have put even more money in the bank.

So, if you shop for recreation, try to find something else to replace the hobby…that doesn't cost money. You might be surprised by how much you can add to your adoption fund.

Possible Monthly Savings: Depends. How impulsive are you?

Transportation

This one may make me unpopular but, could you sell a car?

I'm not saying you must start riding public transportation, but look at how much money you spend on car payments each month. According to Experian Automotive, the average car payment is $471 per month with many car loans stretched out to six and seven years.[3] And many families have two car payments.

When Mark and I first married, we accepted car payments as a way of life. In the first four years, we owned six different vehicles, trading up every time and swallowing a larger car payment with each new car. When we decided to get out of debt, one of the first things we did was sell the car with the most sizeable loan. Then we switched our mentality, and car payments became a thing of the past. We now drive our vehicles until the cost of repair and upkeep is greater than the car's worth. Then we find an older, low-mileage replacement vehicle and pay cash.

Take a close look at your car payments. Could you sell one of those vehicles and buy a good quality used vehicle for $4,000 to $10,000 with lower payments? I promise they exist. In the twelve years since we started paying off our debt, we've bought great vehicles with 60,000 to 70,000 miles for $3,000 to $7,500. And aside from the car I inherited when my grandmother died, they've all been modern-looking cars. My minivan doesn't look or drive like it's fifteen years old.

Over the years of teaching Financial Peace University and doing financial counseling, Mark and I have talked to many people who believed they were so upside down in their car loan that they could never sell and get out from under the debt. I challenge you to pray about it. What seems impossible for man is possible with God. As you sacrifice to make your adoption possible, take steps of faith and trust God for help.

The Boulton family turned in one leased vehicle, sold another car, and bought two less expensive vehicles, allowing them to save hundreds of dollars every month on payments. The dealership told them they would owe money on the leased car, but instead they received a refund check for $3,000. (That check, added to a just-completed fund-raiser, just "happened" to give them $50 more than they needed for their next agency fee. Go, God!)

Or maybe you can get by with one car. Chris and Erin Slay worked at the same hospital so they sold one of their vehicles and carpooled to work every day. The sale gave them $6,500 toward their adoption as well as saving them around $75 a month on insurance costs. Erin said it was an adjustment at first, but they grew to love the daily commute together.

The Smith family sold their second car during their adoption. After paying off the loan they only cleared $100, but the $400 monthly payment was gone and that money went toward the adoption of their daughter. It takes some scheduling finesse, but it's temporary.

Matt Gilliam sold his 1972 black Ford F-150 truck to pay for his and his wife, Jillian's, first home study. He had just acquired a van as a work vehicle and despite his love for the truck, the Gilliams prayed and knew they needed to sell it to move forward and say yes to adoption. They first listed the truck on Facebook and within a week Jillian was contacted by an old middle school friend who had just started a homegrown organic produce business and wanted a "cool" old truck to drive back and forth to the farmer's market. The $3,000 price met her budget and was the exact fee the Gilliams needed for their home study.

"We still miss that truck, and Matt hopes to own one just like it one day again. But God provided exactly what we needed using something that brought us both great joy, so that we could move to something new that will certainly bring us even more joy than that good ol' truck," said Jillian.

So, how much can you save per month? Multiply that number by twelve or even twenty-four to see the impact it will make over the course of your adoption process. Those with a longer process can save even more. Even on our already tight budget, I would estimate we saved at least $2,500 to $3,000 during the year by cutting back expenses. That was enough for both kids' plane tickets home!

Tiffany, with two debt-free adoptions, said,

> We cut off our cable TV, sold our extra vehicle, limited eating out and clothing purchases. We used coupons, raised a garden, cut dryer sheets in half, limited vacations and road trips, shopped clearances sales for necessities, collected spare change, limited movies and rentals (used library card instead), changed home-school curriculum to a less expensive set, cut back on cosmetics, cut back on family

portraits (took snapshots), switched to generic brands for most household and baby items, learned to make my own laundry detergent, cut piano lessons in half, eliminated beauty shop appointments (mommy cuts everybody's hair at home), and bought used items at consignment sales. Through these five adoption attempts, both the failures and the successes, we worked hard, used a lot of our personal savings and retirement funds, prayed for God to provide, and sold a lot of our belongings.

No-Spend Challenge

Sarah and Caleb decided to test their spending habits with the ultimate challenge: "No-Spend November." Before the month began they set these guidelines and published them on their blog:

- Bills get paid
- Tithe as normal
- $220 allotted for gas for both cars
- $320 allotted for groceries
- NO OTHER SPENDING!

The month presented some challenges. When it came time to attend a bridal shower, instead of purchasing a gift, Sarah turned to her craft supplies and made a fun recipe box, filled it with her favorite healthy recipes, and decorated a menu board to go with it. The couple also got creative with their date nights which included a "slumber party" in their loft, an Xbox dance party, and using gift cards that had been given as gifts.

They really stuck to their guns despite burnt-out light bulbs, Caleb's broken belt, and Sarah running out of hairspray. Not surprisingly, they also received quite a few blessings during the month. A $15 Starbucks card allowed them to enjoy some quality morning time together where, instead of buying fancy drinks and blowing the whole thing in one week, they bought regular coffee and stretched it to three coffee dates. When they were pretty much out of grocery money in week three, Caleb received a free turkey at work, which they cooked and made last through the end of the month. Sarah got two free movie tickets for working with United Blood Services through her job.

Even more than the tangible blessings, Sarah and Caleb said they learned some valuable lessons. "Since we have spent more time at home this month, it has really become a safe-haven for us. Before, I rarely wanted to stay in for entertainment; I always wanted go out," Sarah said. "We have broken the habit of just running out to grab something to eat when we are in a rush or just have the desire. Also, our faith grew as we experienced God provide for us on a daily basis. Best of all, Caleb and I spent more quality time together that month than in any other month in our marriage. It's amazing how, when you take away other distractions, you are left with each other and that is incredibly special."

At the end of the month Sarah and Caleb found they had saved $3,889! (They thought maybe they'd save $500.) The crazy thing is that the math doesn't add up. "When we look at our income and look at what we set aside to spend for bills, gas, food, and tithing, it does NOT add up! ALL GOD!" Sarah exclaimed.

Sarah and Caleb think the lessons they learned in delayed satisfaction, creativity, and generosity will keep going and help them add to their adoption savings each month.

CHAPTER NINE
ADOPTION GRANTS

There are several dozen adoption grants available to adoptive families with varying requirements. Most require your home study be complete, but you can apply for a few in the beginning stages of your adoption.

Before you begin applying, it's helpful to understand the three basic types of grants—direct, fund-raising, and matching.

Direct grants are the most desired, but also the most difficult to get. Direct grant organizations, like Show Hope, review applicants and award money outright. Of course these grants are very sought after and usually they receive a high number of applicants. Their ability to award grants is based on their own fund-raising and can change based on funds currently available. Other examples include Gift of Adoption and A Child Waits.

Fund-raising grants give you an account through a nonprofit grant organization to which people can donate. This provides your friends and family with the added benefit of receiving a tax deduction when they donate to your adoption. These are the easiest grants to qualify for since the grant organization is not giving you money out of its pocket. I tell every adoptive family who applies for this type of grants to have at least one avenue where people can donate money and receive a tax deduction. I guarantee at least a few people are going to want to donate toward your adoption, why not give them the tax break as well? Also, several fund-raisers work better if you're attached to a 501(c)(3). Lifesong for Orphans is one example.

When applying for a fund-raising grant you may notice some wording on the application that sets off some red flags. Something like, "All funds generated become the property of (GRANT ORG), a 501(c)(3) charity. Due to IRS regulations, we cannot guarantee all funds received will benefit your personal adoption expenses. We make a best effort to afford you your requested grant."

Don't be too alarmed. IRS regulations require nonprofits to retain discretion over the use of donor funds and so most organizations include this wording on their applications or receipts. They actually have to in order to keep their nonprofit status. So double check with the organization, but most will tell you that any funds received with your name will go to your account.

Some fund-raising grant organizations charge a small administrative fee, maybe 5 to 10 percent, but there are enough that do not that you should try to get one with no overhead fee.

Matching grants are basically a combination of direct and fundraising. The grant organization asks you to fund-raise and provides the tax benefit to your donors. Then they match a certain dollar amount of donations received. They often provide you with sample fund-raising letters, or you can find some on other parents' blogs. Lifesong for Orphans also provides matching grants to some families.

With both fund-raising and matching grants the organization pays the money directly to "service providers," usually your adoption agency. Some grants will pay money to travel agents. Some may, with receipts, reimburse you for expenses already paid to providers.

Most require the same basic financial information so you'll save time if you gather all the information before you start. Because many of the applications are similar, you'll also save time if you fill them out in batches.

Here's a general checklist of items you may need to send in with your application:

• Final home study

- Tax returns (one to two years)
- List of assets/net worth
- Monthly cash flow budget
- Recent pay stubs
- Recent bank statements (checking, savings, retirement)
- Your expected adoption costs
- Amount you have available to pay for your adoption
- Personal testimony/statement of faith
- Adoption testimony (why you want to adopt)
- Pictures of your family
- Information on child you're adopting (if you have it)
- References—pastor, employer, friend, caseworker, and so on

While it is time-consuming and daunting, don't neglect this process because grants could provide quite a chunk of money for your adoption.

Many people ask, "What are the grant organizations looking for when they award money?" I wish there was a magic answer that would guarantee your selection. The truth is that the award process is based on many different things and it varies by organization. But there are several common factors.

The need of the child: Some organizations will place families adopting older or special needs children higher on the list. Some grants are specific to only these types of adoption. The term "special needs" can mean a lot of things and sometimes refers to any adoption of a child over the age of five. If you see a grant organization that is only for special needs adoptions, ask for their specific definition of that term.

The financial need of the family: Obviously if your annual household income is $300,000 you're probably not going to be high on the list. This is a tricky one and is where a lot of discernment comes in on the part of the grant organizations. Maybe you have a decent yearly income but you're still paying off student loans and other debt. Or maybe you're like we were, and had a good income for the previous year but your situation has changed. All I can say is to be honest and detailed in your application. Most organizations offer a spot for you to note any special circumstances that should be considered.

Grant organizations want to know how much you are going to be able to contribute to the adoption and what you are doing to raise funds. If your monthly cash flow budget shows you are making two car payments, a boat payment, and own a vacation home, they'll be wondering what you're willing to sacrifice in order to make your adoption dream come true.

Church support: Some grant organizations require a pastor referral and will want to know if your church is going to financially support you or be actively involved in helping you raise funds for your adoption.

There is a list of grants in the appendix to this book. And, while not exhaustive, it does contain the most well-known grants. For a complete list, visit Resources4Adoption.com.

Fund-Raising Letters

If you receive a fund-raising grant or a matching grant, you'll need to write a fund-raising letter. Most grant organizations provide a sample letter and may give you some specific language to use for the donation instructions.

Write your letter from your heart, and reflect your family and your journey. Many families include a few frequently asked questions about adoption and why it costs so much.

In your letter, you should not only ask for donations to your adoption fund but also use this opportunity to ask if people can help you raise money in other ways. If they cannot give financially, can they help you with a garage sale or spaghetti dinner fund-raiser? Do they have a talent, like photography, that they could use to help you raise funds?

Don't forget that even more important than financial help is the need for prayer warriors. We received a fund-raising grant for our adoption, and we used the opportunity to ask our friends and family to pray for us and for Wendemagegn, Beza, and their grandmother.

Even if you don't have a fund-raising grant, you can still send out letters. Just be sure people know their donation is a gift directly to you and not eligible for a tax donation.

Kenny and Catherine Besk sent out about one hundred letters and received over $15,000 in straight financial gifts toward their adoption. While they received three gifts of over $1,000, most people donated between $20 and $200. It all adds up.

Jillian and Matt Gilliam were hesitant to send out a general donation request letter but then they received a $2,500 matching grant from Hand in Hand. They sent out fifty-five letters and ended up receiving $4,700 in donations for a total grant of $7,200.

Though their letter was more a family update than a donation request, I love what Kim did. The family included a small, self-addressed stamped note card to their future daughter that people could use to share a note or verse for her scrapbook. Kim says that some people included a donation when they mailed the card back.

Sample Fund-Raising Letter for Domestic Adoption

Dear Friends,

For almost two years now, we have been in the adoption process. In the beginning, we considered an international adoption, public adoption, and foster care. We researched several options and agencies and even went to informational meetings on some of these options.

We decided on a domestic infant adoption for several reasons. The most important being that this is the way God has led us. Another reason is that we want to learn how to be parents from the ground up.

The application and home study process lasted a year and a half for us. During this time, we were very serious about paying off some of our debt. We were approved by the agency in [month / year].

As we get closer to the day when our child will join our family, we want to update the special people in our lives about this process. Through this process, our hearts have changed from wanting to add a child to our family to wanting to be a family for our child.

Currently, we are waiting to be chosen by a birth mother (and possibly the father) to raise a child or to be assigned a child through our agency. This is an exciting time because we literally could get a phone call any day that we have been picked *or* that our child is at the hospital waiting to be picked up. It is also a bit of an uneasy time, for exactly the same reason. We have been in the waiting stage for four months now. However, we have not just been idly sitting around waiting for this life-changing phone call. Life continues as normal with our jobs, family and friends. But, it's also completely different because each day we wonder, "Could today be the day?" We are thankful that we have confidence in the Lord's perfect timing and know that it will happen exactly when it's supposed to.

While we wait, we have seen the Lord provide for this adoption through fund-raising and donations. So far, we have raised $_____ of our $_____ goal. God is truly a wonderful Provider! We are so thankful for the people God has used to support us so far. We know that our baby is already loved so much!

Because we hope our child will be coming home soon, we wanted to ask you to pray with us and prayerfully consider financially supporting the remainder of our adoption costs. These are the ways you can help:

1. **Prayer**—Please pray God will tenderly care for our child and his or her birth family, that God will prepare us for the upcoming changes to our family, and that God will give us wisdom, discernment, and insight as we raise our son or daughter to know Jesus Christ.

2. **Financial support**—Will you please consider making a tax-deductible donation to help us pay the remaining $_____ in adoption expenses?

If you would like to be a part of God bringing our baby to Himself through our family, you can send your gift between now and [end date] to the address below. [Briefly describe the grant organization or agency you have partnered with, if any, and any rules they may have for donations.]

Mail checks to:

[Provide ADDRESS]

Thank you for investing in the Kingdom through prayer and finances—it will be an investment with an eternal return! (Matt 6:20) We'll give you an update with a picture of our baby and details as we receive them. Please pray this entire process will glorify God and fulfill His purposes!

To stay updated, stay tuned to our blog.

In Christ,

Matthew and Tricia

Sample Fund-Raising Letter for International Adoption

Dear Friends,

We would like to share some very exciting news with you.

We're adopting!

Yes, I know we said we were done after having two children but, surprise, God changed our minds.

A few months ago we began the process to adopt a boy from Ethiopia, which is where God led us after much prayer and research. We both have a deep love for this beautiful country already and have found many Ethiopian families in our community that we can stay connected to.

We do not know him yet. What we do know is this:

He may never have known the warm and loving embrace of a mother or the joy of a piggy-back ride from a father. He doesn't know what it feels like to be tucked in next to his favorite stuffed animal and kissed goodnight—warm and safe. He hasn't had a mom or dad to kiss his boo-boos and cheer him on as he accomplishes new things. He doesn't know that he can be *anything* he wants to be when he grows up.

You can help provide this for him.

We cannot wait to bring him home! No words can capture our excitement at the idea of bringing this new little guy into our family. The kids are equally excited to have a new little brother.

We want you to become part of our adoption. First, we would love a group of family and friends dedicated to praying for us through this journey. We would also ask you to cover our son in prayer, wherever he may be. God knows and he already knows that he is ours.

Second, we are fund-raising to help provide for the financial cost of the adoption. We have worked diligently to trim our household expenses and find the money for the approximately $_____ we will need. These costs include our home study (where the state approves us to adopt), agency fees, attorney costs, government paperwork, background checks, and for the care of our son while he is in-country. We also have to travel to [country] two times—once for court and once to bring him home. We will also be doing some fund-raisers like a garage sale in an effort to do everything we can.

At this point we estimate that we still need to raise about $_____. Will you prayerfully consider making a financial gift to help us bring our son home? You can give him a family. We trust that God will provide the funds needed to complete this adoption. One way may be through people like you.

You can give two ways. You can make a direct gift to us by check or through the PayPal link on our blog (address below).

[Briefly describe the grant organization or agency you have partnered with, if any, and any rules they may have for donations.]

Or you can mail checks to:

[Provide ADDRESS]

If you cannot give financially, there may still be a way for you to help. In the coming months we will be hosting a few fund-raising events, including a garage sale and a pancake breakfast. We'll need lots of helping hands!

We are also doing an auction and collecting donations from friends, family, and local businesses. If you have goods or services that you could donate, we would love to have you participate.

If you're interested in either of those opportunities, just send us an e-mail and we'll follow up with you. Please contact us if you have any questions, need alternative methods of contribution, or would just like to chat. We would absolutely love to hear from each and every one of you!

Thank you for taking the time to let us share our journey with you.

Sincerely,

Scott and Emily

"I tell you the truth, when you did it to one of the least of these my brothers and sisters, you were doing it to me!" —Matthew 25:40

CHAPTER TEN
EMPLOYER BENEFITS

In the last five years there has been a growing trend in employers offering adoption benefits. The Dave Thomas Foundation for Adoption (DTFA) surveys and tracks these companies, each year publishing its 100 Best Adoption-Friendly Workplaces list.

Not surprisingly, the number-one company on the 2013 list was The Wendy's Company, which offers up to $25,300 and six weeks of paid leave to adoptive parents.[1]

You can download the 100 Best Adoption-Friendly Workplaces list from the DTFA (adoptionfriendlyworkplace.org) website as well as view a page of 327 companies that offer benefits of some kind. The list doesn't include the U.S. military, which may reimburse qualified adoption expenses of $2,000 per adoptive child under eighteen years of age and up to $5,000 if more than one child is adopted.[2]

There are two types of adoption benefits: paid leave and financial assistance.

Adoptive parents are covered under the U.S. Department of Labor Family and Medical Leave Act (FMLA), but that only entitles you to unpaid, job-protected leave if you work for a qualifying company. Ask if your company offers *paid* maternity leave. The amount often depends on how long you've worked for the company. If they do, check if the policy mentions adoptive parents. If not, don't assume that means you won't be included, but do ask someone in the human resources department for clarification. It could just be that they didn't think to include the wording in the employee benefits package. The average paid leave offered by adoption-friendly employers is six weeks, with many offering unpaid leave beyond that required by FMLA.

Financial assistance may range from $500 to $25,000 with an average reimbursement of $6,000.[3] Some employers pay it in a lump sum directly to the employee, and some reimburse specific expenses. Often it is only paid after the adoption is finalized. If paid directly to the employee, it is not subject to federal income tax withholding (Section 137 of the Internal Revenue Code).[4]

Either benefit may require you to have been employed by the company for a certain length of time before you are eligible.

If your company doesn't offer one or both of these adoption benefits, take heart. Of the employers completing the DTFA survey, 55 percent said they added adoption benefits because of employee requests. You might be the employee who starts it all.

Sometimes all it takes is one person asking. DTFA makes advocating for employer adoption benefits super simple by offering a free kit on their website. The kit includes helpful information and a DVD with document templates to use while advocating and to help implement and announce any new benefits.

Talk to human resources and ask them if the company has ever considered adoption benefits. If so, why did they end up not offering them? Who supported the idea? Who didn't? Use that information to help you as you advocate for benefits.

How Adoption Leave Benefits the Company

- Benefit trends—Since 2007, when DTFA began tracking employer adoption benefits, there has been a significant increase in both the quantity and quality of the programs. To stay competitive, companies want to offer attractive benefit packages.
- Employee loyalty—Employee satisfaction means increased productivity. Parents who receive adoption benefits most likely have a renewed sense of loyalty. Even employees who aren't adopting appreciate that the company recognizes the importance of adoption.

- Equity—Women who give birth typically receive maternity benefits, including paid time off. Adoptive mothers should get that same support. Likewise dads should receive the same benefits whether their family was formed through pregnancy or adoption.
- Low cost—Less than 1 percent of a company's employees will use adoption benefits during a year.
- Giving back to the community—By offering adoption benefits, the company shows that it cares about families, which ultimately betters the community. Not that you want your adoption to become a public relations tool, but companies do enjoy looking good.

Make It Personal

Share your adoption story. If you know other employees who have adopted, talk to them and ask them how having adoption benefits would have helped. Include that in your request. If there are others in the adoption process, get them to include a brief story as well.

Do the Work for Them

If you want a section on adoption benefits added to the employee handbook, write it for them. In my time in the corporate world I found that the managers loved it when I presented an idea with the action item already done. If they approved it, there was minimal work for them to pass it on for implementation. The DTFA toolkit DVD provides a template proposal ready for you to customize and present. If you call DTFA they can also provide examples of what other similar-sized companies offer in terms of financial compensation and paid leave.

Present It to the Right Person

In most cases I would start with your direct supervisor. He or she may not have direct decision-making capability, but instead frame it as "I'm interested in proposing adding adoption benefits to our benefits package and I'd really love your input. Would you be willing to look over some items I've prepared?" Your supervisor may provide helpful insight in how to phrase your presentation or give you an idea of what other questions may arise. Ask him or her if you have permission to take the proposal to the next person in the supervisor chain or if it needs to come from him or her. Your supervisor may tell you to start with someone in the human resources department.

Even if your employer turns your request down, know that perhaps you have planted a seed and somewhere down the line the company's policy will change and benefit other families.

CHAPTER ELEVEN
SACRIFICES AND SECOND INCOMES

Turn Clutter and Excess to Cash

Look around your house and your garage to find things you don't use anymore, specifically the bigger items. Do you have exercise equipment that spends most of its time draped with clothes or old video game systems your kids no longer play? Gather the items up and sell them—either on Craigslist or eBay. (Research prices on both sites to see which method works better. Obviously, sell items too big to ship on Craigslist.)

You might also consider things you use but are willing to sacrifice for the greater good of bringing a child into your family—the flat-screen TV, boat or recreational vehicles, or timeshare.

Next gather the smaller stuff. If you haven't used something in six months (twelve on the outside), sell it! Start a pile in your garage and spend a little time each day sorting through an area of your house. Tackle one closet at a time. You can clean out a closet in a couple of hours. Plus, you'll feel better when you've put everything away in a neat, organized fashion. (Or maybe that's just me. I am a little obsessive-compulsive.)

Even if it takes you a month, go through the house and garage and build a pile. The goal is to sell all of it at a garage sale, which is covered in detail in chapter 13.

Sometimes sacrifice means parting with something that you do use frequently, but can live without. Lee owned a fishing boat that he loved. Even though the boat was used frequently for either fishing or taking evening boat rides with his wife, Jeannie, they decided to sell it and use the $2,000 for their adoption expenses. "I miss the boat, but my son more than makes up for it," Jeannie said.

eBay Basics

Selling stuff on eBay does take time, but it's easy to do from home. All you need is a digital camera and shipping materials. If you plan on selling a large quantity of items, buy an inexpensive postage scale so you can weigh packages at home and label them for shipping. You can order free shipping supplies from the USPS website as well as print postage. This saves you time and allows you to simply drop off the already paid packages without standing in line. Or you can schedule a pickup at your home.

If you've never used eBay before, this site shows you all the basics—pages.ebay.com/sellerinformation/index.html.

Not sure if you should sell an item on eBay? Type your item into the search box to get current listings. Then scroll down on the left and click the "Completed" box. This will show you only closed auctions. Prices in green show you what the item sold for. Remember you'll be paying eBay and PayPal fees as well as the time spent for listing something. I typically don't waste my time with anything less than $5. You can also sell similar items in "lots" and they will go for more money as well as take less time to list. For example, when finished with my maternity clothes I separated them into several groups—business, casual, and special occasion and sold them in lots for between $60 to $120.

If you've had some experience with eBay, you can potentially turn it into a second source of income. A lot of people are quite successful buying and reselling used items online.

During our adoption Mark bought a variety of items at thrift stores and resold them, some golf clubs and miscellaneous household items. He seems to have an eye for what might be worth something and will check eBay on his phone while he's right there in the thrift store. He continues today with a little less regularity, but it's kind of a fun challenge for him. He likes to focus on a few particular items such as wireless routers and remote controls. Sounds weird right? But he learned what to look for and finds remote controls he purchases for $2 to $5, then resells for $20 or more. One remote even went for $75! I like it because routers and remote controls take up way less space in my house than golf clubs.

Second Incomes

Is there a way you could make additional income above what you make now? Maybe you have a job that gives you the opportunity to work overtime?

Or could you temporarily take on a second job? If you delivered pizzas a couple of nights a week, you could stash away $500 to $600 a month.

What about a newspaper route? Depending on the size of your route, which would depend on the time you could devote, you could make $300 to $1,000 a month.

Maybe you're a stay-at-home mom with young children and working outside the home isn't feasible. Could you provide childcare for one or two kids during the week? Check your state laws, but most states will allow you to care for a certain number of children before you must become licensed. Depending upon your area, you could earn $100 to $200 each week per child for providing full-time care. Or maybe you could offer "mom's-day-out" babysitting once a week to other stay-at-home moms.

Waiting tables is pretty good money, especially if you can work the weekend dinner shifts. Working at a mid-range chain restaurant can bring in $50 to $100 a night in tips plus the small, and I do mean small, hourly wage.

Or you might decide to return to work to help pay adoption expenses. Jodie was a stay-at-home mom to her three kids before she and her husband began their Ethiopian adoption process. She returned to work full-time. After childcare expenses, they saved three quarters of her salary for their adoption, and their son came home in November 2008. Jodie took some time off to spend with the family before returning to work. She eventually went back to staying at home full-time.

Of course, you want to be above board and fair to any potential employer. They invest time and money with any new employee. Some industries have a high turnover rate but it's unfair to present yourself to a potential employer as a long-term employee if you know that you're going to leave in six to nine months.

My friend, Jen, is a hair stylist. She held a couple of hair-cutting events and asked people to donate to her family's tax-deductible grant fund. They received $800 in donations.

If your adoption journey takes you through the holiday months, consider taking on a seasonal job those last two or three months. Most retail stores, as well as retail distribution centers like Amazon, hire extra holiday help. Start looking and applying in October.

Or maybe you have a job skill you can use outside of your regular work hours.

Over the years, I have taken freelance design jobs as an extra source of income. In the beginning, we used the income to pay off debt; then we used it to fund extras like new furniture or vacations that weren't in our regular budget. I never advertised for clients; they came to me by word-of-mouth from friends, coworkers, and family. Sometimes, I'd go months without any jobs, then have one or two, then nothing again for a while.

A few weeks after Mark left his job, the freelance work trickled in and then it piled up! On several jobs, I earned more than $1,000 to $1,500, which we put into our adoption savings. This was a huge encouragement to us that, indeed, God was rewarding our commitment. Overall, my freelance work probably added $8,000 to our adoption fund.

One adoptive mom is also an amazing photographer who helped found a cooperative of photographers who help celebrate the beauty of adoption by donating their services to new adoptive families. She started a local photography workshop for moms interested in learning how to better capture those everyday moments in their kids' lives. Highly in demand, she put together an online workshop and has used it to raise funds for their adoption.

Jo Anna Crawford and her husband Scott both work as pharmacists, but Jo Anna usually only worked twenty hours a week. During their three-year adoption process Jo Anna took on extra shifts when possible and contributed approximately $10,000 extra toward their expenses to adopt two boys from the Philippines.

While his wife made leather cuff bracelets, Matt Gilliam took on various handyman jobs that allowed them to cover their application fees.

Several adoptive moms have been quite successful making and selling handmade items on sites like Etsy. There are lots of examples in the next chapter.

You and your spouse, if you're married, need to reach an agreement on this issue. Taking on additional work at the expense of your marriage or your family is not worth the money. If you're a single parent, an extra job simply may not work. But don't worry, you still have lots of options.

After you reexamine your budget and apply for grants, the gap between your funds and adoption costs is the perfect opportunity for creative fund-raising.

CHAPTER TWELVE
FUND-RAISING

For some the mere mention of the word *fund-raising* causes a shudder. We've all had to either sell or buy our fair share of frozen cookie dough, overpriced gift wrap, and magazine subscriptions from our children or the neighbor kids.

Some people are adamantly opposed to fund-raising for their adoption. They assume it means begging for money. But keep an open mind. There are a variety of things you can do to earn funds toward your adoption. Some involve a more direct ask, but there are plenty of fun, no-pressure ideas as well.

Ultimately as Christ followers we are called to share in one another's burdens as well as joy. Adoption is both. There is the great task of paying for the adoption and the great joy in giving a child a forever family. This is what the church (the body of believers) should be about. Giving generously to those in need.

> And all the believers met together in one place and shared everything they had. They sold their property and possessions and shared the money with those in need. They worshiped together at the Temple each day, met in homes for the Lord's Supper, and shared their meals with great joy and generosity—all the while praising God and enjoying the goodwill of all the people. And each day the Lord added to their fellowship those who were being saved. (Acts 2: 44-47a)

Chris and Erin Slay came to realize this during their adoption process.

> We started this venture wanting to do it all ourselves—fund-raise ourselves, redo our budget ourselves. It wasn't until we were called out by a friend who wanted to help that we realized we were keeping others from the blessing of adoption if we didn't let them help us. Not everyone feels called to adopt by bringing a child home, but many feel called to be involved in the process. Open up, be honest about your financial situation, but do everything you can on your own before begging for handouts.

The Pros and Cons of Fund-Raising

Before you begin the next few chapters on fund-raising, consider some pros and cons of asking for help to cover your expenses.

Pros

Raises awareness—Welcoming other people into your adoption journey allows you to share your heart for adoption and your heart for the orphan. Many people are unaware of the orphan crisis, here and abroad, and the need for loving solutions for U.S. birth moms who want to place their child for adoption. Even if others never give to your adoption, you never know how far this influence will reach. You may find one of these families later adopting themselves.

Allows others to be obedient—Remember that scripture about caring for the orphan and widow? If adoption isn't for everyone, what is one other way they can care for orphans? Financially supporting your adoption gives your friends and family the opportunity to carry out God's call.

Teaches humility—Asking for help is hard, especially financial help. But what if you didn't look at fund-raising as asking your friends? Because really you're asking God to provide for your adoption. It is

God who supplies all our needs, but sometimes He uses others to do it. How can people help if they don't know the need?

Makes adoption possible—Quite frankly many people would never be able to adopt without fund-raising. Even if they take out loans, those are limited, grants are limited, and many of the biggest adoption advocates are those already pouring out their financial gifts on others or working in ministry. Without fund-raising many adoptions would simply not happen.

Cons

Hard work—Fund-raising is labor intensive, whether it's sorting donations and preparing for a garage sale, or the perseverance to blog, Facebook and tweet about your efforts. Hopefully you have a village of people who want to help you.

The questions—You're going to get a lot of questions and a few insensitive comments. Friends might ask "Why does a kid cost so much?" It's a good time for you to use some positive adoption language as well as educate them on why adoption is expensive. Explain about agency fees and paperwork and travel. Be open and honest.

Accountability—If adoption donations are coming straight to you, versus to a grant organization, you need to be faithful about making sure that money *only* goes toward adoption expenses. Not "we're going to have another kid" expenses like a bigger car, nursery décor, and clothes, but agency fees, paperwork costs, and so on. Consider opening up a separate savings account just for these funds.

Scrutiny—If you're asking for money you are opening yourself up to scrutiny. You may not want to send out a fund-raising letter and then leave on a ten-day cruise two weeks later. This is especially hard in the digital age where we tend to spew our every move via Twitter and Facebook. What if that cruise is a work perk that isn't costing you a cent? What a blessing! Just be sure to mention that when you post all the touristy pictures. Better yet, don't post them. Also, be vocal about what you're doing to help pay for the adoption—things like trimming your budget or taking on second jobs.

Backlash—Be prepared for the "If you can't afford it then you shouldn't be doing it" comments. Who criticizes may even surprise and hurt you. First, let them know you would never want them to feel obligated to give or participate in your fund-raiser. You might also say something like, "We're working really hard to fund this adoption ourselves but many people have asked how they can help."

Managing Your Expectations

I've talked with several families where fund-raising has caused some hard feelings between family members. One woman was disappointed that her financially well-off sister did not give toward their adoption at all. It strained their relationship for several years.

My advice? *Expect nothing.* If they don't give, you won't be disappointed. If they do, you'll feel especially blessed. Let people know that you would never want them to feel obligated and that their friendship and prayers mean more to you than any financial gift.

The Direct Approach

In chapter 10 I talked about sending out fund-raising letters in the context of grants. But even without a grant, many families choose to start first by asking friends and family to donate toward their adoption expenses.

Being vulnerable and admitting you don't have the resources on your own takes guts. So why consider it? Curtis Honeycutt, a waiting adoptive father, wrote a great guest post for my blog. Having fund-raised over $25,000 for their adoption of a child from Ghana, he has great perspective. First, he said, the direct approach will often "give you the biggest bang for your buck." Sending out letters and using social media to ask for funds doesn't take as much time as organizing and having a multiday garage sale and endless party fund-raisers. You only have so much "vision capital," as Curtis calls it, with your friends and family. Endless requests to buy products might use that up and not get you the same dollar amount they would have donated if you had just asked.

Also, some typical fund-raisers reinforce our "cultural consumeristic tendencies." Your friends buy your adoption T-shirt, you get $10, and they feel good about themselves knowing they helped. End of story. But that $10 is a drop in the bucket and then those friends are done. Instead, Curtis suggests framing your fund-raising within the larger vision. What they receive in turn for their donation is twofold. One, they get the lifetime feeling of knowing they directly contributed to giving a child a forever family. Two, they helped grow your family through adoption. Curtis said,

> The frustrating thing we found with this approach is that many people who we really thought we could count on for a generous donation stayed on the bench when it came time to respond. Honestly this was pretty hurtful. On the other hand, we were bowled over with gratitude by receiving surprising donations in large amounts from people we didn't know all that well or people we knew were making a big sacrifice. The difference? The people close to us who sat out didn't resonate with our vision for fund-raising, but the people who stepped up really did. What you need to do as the fund-raiser is find the people who deeply care about orphans and understand their role in healing this broken place in the world.[1]

Odds are you are going to have to do a combination of things. So how do you know if fund-raising is right for you and what kind of fund-raisers to do?

There is no easy answer. The decision is deeply personal. Cover it, like any major decision, in prayer. If you do not feel at peace about fund-raising, then don't. Pursue other ideas like bringing in a second income or selling things you own.

These next few chapters provide a variety of fund-raising ideas and illustrate that there are creative ways to pay for your adoption in addition to outright asking for money. The samples included may even spark your own creative idea.

For example, one couple didn't feel comfortable with most of the traditional fund-raising ideas. The couple is active in the horse and rodeo circuit and got inspired to raffle the horse off. They spent seven months selling $50 raffle tickets by advertising on Craigslist, on horse sale websites, in magazines, and with flyers in tack and feed stores. They attended every local horse event they could, selling tickets in their booth with the horse nearby. They raised $24,000, nearly five times the amount they could have sold the horse for, and gave the first $1,000 to a nonprofit organization feeding kids in Africa.

This couple did something that felt right to them. (Be aware, however, that giveaways or raffles can present a bit of a problem. If they meet the legal IRS definition of "gaming" they are subject to state gambling laws. For a list of raffle laws by state, go to rafflefaq.com /united-states-raffle-laws/. Please read more about this in chapter 15.)

Selecting Your Fund-Raisers

Before you select a fund-raising option, spend some time thinking through these four things.

Time—How much time can you spend fund-raising? How many months or years do you have left in your adoption process? A single parent or a couple where both work full-time is going to have less time to fund-raise. Select fund-raisers that don't have as large of a time commitment. If you're two months away from bringing home your child, look for quick, big impact fund-raisers like a garage sale.

Help—Do you have friends and family who will help you put together a pancake breakfast or organize a 5k? Many of the fund-raisers are doable on your own, but some require you to have some extra hands on board. Don't be afraid to ask for help. You'd be surprised at how many people are willing to pitch in when they know what you need.

Audience—You undoubtedly have different circles of friends. You may have work friends, church friends, and neighborhood friends. Different fund-raisers will appeal to different groups. For example, the karaoke fund-raiser mentioned in chapter 14 was created to appeal specifically to Kenny Besk's law enforcement coworkers. If you have mostly young families with small kids in your circle, then a fund-raising dinner that requires them to get babysitters may not be the best option. But a spaghetti dinner with a bounce house for the kids? Perfect! It's about finding the right idea for each group.

Reach—How wide is your advertising reach? If you have a blog and are connected in social media, some fund-raisers will be easier for you. Also consider the reach of friends and family who you know will be willing to extend your reach by sharing your fund-raisers with their friends and family. If your church is super supportive of your adoption and will allow you to promote your fund-raisers, then certain ideas, like the envelope fund-raiser, may be a great fit.

Thank-You Notes Are Priceless

No matter what type of fund-raising you do there is one step you must not forget—thank-you notes. Write one *every* time you can. Even if the gift was $5, donors deserve a handwritten thank-you note.

Most fund-raising grant organizations will provide you with a list of your donors unless the donor asked to remain anonymous. If you're doing a Facebook fund-raiser and getting donations from people that you don't have addresses for, then, at a minimum, send them a private Facebook message of thanks. Some people will post a note of thanks on the donor's Facebook wall, but remember that not everyone may want their donation being made public.

Tax Implications

Remember that if you are bringing in extra income through your fund-raisers, you are required to pay federal and state income taxes as well as FICA on anything over $600. The income is classified as self-employment income and so there are multiple tax implications. Consult a tax service or licensed CPA to estimate what percentage you should be setting aside to pay taxes. Cash gifts given to you are not taxable unless a single gift (from one person) exceeds $14,000.

CHAPTER THIRTEEN
EVENT FUND-RAISERS

Event fund-raisers are not new. I imagine we've all participated in a car wash or two at some point for school and club activities. You can adapt many, if not all, of these same ideas for your adoption fund.

Garage Sales

Garage sales have one of the biggest return potentials in the shortest amount of time, and you can do them multiple times. They are a great way to get those initial funds that you need to get through the application and home study process. It's also a great example of a fund-raiser that isn't asking for money!

I am always purging closets of toys, clothes, and junk. Most often, it goes to the thrift store in small batches. But at the beginning of our adoption, we'd built up quite a pile in the garage, and so we opted for a garage sale—something we do every couple of years. I think the most we'd made at any previous garage sale was $300 to $400. But any amount helps, right?

We joined forces with our friends, the Slonigers, who were ten months into their adoption process, and another adoptive family. We knew we'd not only collect more stuff, but we'd have a lot more fun doing it with friends.

First, pick a date for the sale. Give yourself at *least* six to eight weeks to plan and collect donations. Avoid holiday weekends because many people are out of town or have family plans. The weather may come into consideration as well. Living in Phoenix, people have garage sales year-round but your location may be different. Consider having a two-day sale—Friday/Saturday sales are popular in our town, and, surprisingly, we made the majority of our money on Friday.

I designed a simple flyer on the computer using a Microsoft Publisher template, converted it to PDF, and sent it via e-mail to all our friends, asking for any donations of used furniture, clothing, and household items. Basically we pleaded to take their junk off their hands. We listed multiple drop-off locations (our three homes and a work location) and offered to pick up items as well. If you don't have a large vehicle, see if a friend will help pick up furniture and other large items.

While you're advertising for donations, solicit volunteers to help with day-before preparations and sale-day support. Keep a list of people who offer to help so you can call them when it's time.

Ask your friends to tell their friends. Spread the word on your blog, Facebook, and Twitter. We received stuff from people we didn't know who heard about it from mutual friends. And neither of us was even on social media at the time.

At the end of six weeks, the donations filled up two bays of our garage, a storage room, a carport, and the back patio of the Slonigers' house. One friend was selling a furnished vacation rental home and gave us some really nice items. We had larger items like beds, dining room tables, and mattresses, but the majority were smaller items—clothes, toys, books, small electronics, and tools. You name it, we had it!

If you have really nice larger items like furniture, you will probably get more money by selling the item on Craigslist. As soon as you receive a big-ticket item, take good pictures and list it for a fair price. If the item doesn't sell, put it out at the garage sale.

Dave and Amy had one garage sale that made over $2,000 and then decided to do another a year later after they were matched with a birth mother. They asked friends for donations, but then Dave had a genius idea while scrolling through Craigslist. What do all those people having garage sales do with their leftover stuff? Many of them either list it for free haul-away the next day or take it to a thrift store.

So Dave created an e-mail template explaining the adoption fund-raiser garage sale and asking if he could pick up garage sale leftovers. He contacted people listing garage sales in the weeks before their sale. At least ten people said yes and helped them bring in $4,400 on their second sale.

Craigslist also has a "Free" section where you may find some sellable items. Oftentimes people just put stuff on their curb and it's first come, first served.

Think about the best location for your sale. Most people will have it at their house, and that's certainly the easiest. We had three houses to choose from and we decided to have it at the Slonigers' because they live in a little higher-priced community, are within two blocks of an elementary school and major resort and golf course. On that Friday every mom dropping their child off at school saw our signs and many of them came by and helped make that first day hugely successful. The Slonigers also had the majority of the larger items at their house already.

If you can't have garage sales in your neighborhood due to homeowner association rules or city restrictions, see if you can hold one in the parking lot of the local school or a church. If your neighborhood or city has a pre-advertised garage sale weekend, for sure you want to have it at the same time. The subdivision group sales always get more traffic.

Also check with your city and see if you are required to have a permit or if they have sign restrictions. You certainly don't want to get shut down halfway through your sale.

Hopefully you'll have a ton of items, which means you're going to need lots of tables. Check with friends for folding tables you can borrow for sale day. If you belong to a church, they might loan them to you. You can always rent them, but free is better. To display items, we used six six-foot tables plus the surfaces of some of the furniture we were selling.

All day Thursday, we arranged and priced stuff with the help of a couple of friends. Don't price stuff too high, but don't go too low either. Generally, you'll sell stuff for less than half of the retail price. Make the prices easy to add mentally like in 25-cent increments.

If you're wavering on a price, go with the higher amount because people will likely bargain, and then you can lower your price. Batch price some categories that have a large number of items. For example, sell all videos for 50 cents, all books for $1. Mark the category price on a sign by the items (grouped together), and keep a list of those categories and prices for the cashier's reference. This will save you the time of pricing every individual video.

Our pile of donations included at least fifteen lawn-size garbage bags full of clothes—totally overwhelming. We sorted through them and grouped them by baby, kid's, men's, and women's. The high-end, name-brand items we pulled out, priced separately, and hung on a clothes rack. On the day of the sale, we laid plastic tarps in the yard and put the clothes in the sorted piles. We priced everything at 50 cents each *or* let shoppers fill an eight-gallon trash bag for $5. Our main goal was to sell as many clothes as possible. Don't bother folding clothing—it will be undone within the first thirty minutes. Our piles didn't stay sorted very well either, partly because we had them spaced closely together.

Create signs on bright-colored poster board for the neighborhood and cover all the major nearby intersections with detailed signs—for example, "HUGE GARAGE SALE Fri/Sat 6 a.m.–noon" and an arrow. Using the same color poster board, put smaller arrow-only signs to guide shoppers through the neighborhood to your house.

A few days before your sale, put a garage sale ad on Craigslist with a detailed list of some of the larger furniture and electronic items. We had people come looking for specific items listed, so it definitely works.

You can also create a Facebook event for your sale and invite local friends to share it with others.

Recruit help for the day of the sale—preferably friends with garage sale and negotiating experience. We ladies left the husbands to negotiate the electronics and tools because we had no idea what stuff was worth. Arm everyone with a black marker. Set up one cashier station with a table and cash box. If a customer negotiates a better price on an item with one of your helpers, instruct your helpers to cross off the price and write the new one on the tag.

Make a big sign that says "Adoption Fund-Raiser." We found people haggled less when they realized the money went to a good cause. Some even gave us extra money or had us keep the change from their purchase. The sign also allowed us to share our adoption story with lots of people. If you already have a referral picture, put a copy by the cashier or on a poster.

You can make a few extra dollars by selling drinks, such as coffee, water, or soda. If you have elementary aged kids, this is a great way to get them involved. Some people have sold donuts and various baked goods, but check your local food handling code. Some states have exemptions for small-scale events for nonprofits and schools and that may include your function.

We sold a *ton* of stuff that first weekend, but we had so much left over at the end of Saturday that we had another sale at our house the following weekend. Even then, we didn't sell everything. Instead of hanging on to it for another weekend, we passed everything on to a friend hosting her own garage sale a few weeks later. In hindsight, I might have held on to the leftovers and had another sale a few months later but in the exhaustion of the moment I just wanted the stuff *gone*!

If you have big-ticket items like furniture left over, put them back up on Craigslist.

How much can you make? Depending on the scale of your sale, you can raise a few hundred to a few thousand dollars. In four days, we made $5,200. The work was exhausting, but fun and well worth the effort.

Other Garage Sale Successes

More than thirty families donated items to the Hendricks family for their garage sale. Kevin and Abby told shoppers they were adopting and, instead of pricing each item, asked people to give them a donation. They accepted most reasonable offers and found many people gave more than they would have normally paid. They did, however, reject the fifty-cent offer for the couch.

The Hendricks had so much stuff that the garage sale lasted three weekends. By the third weekend, they marked *everything* down to 25 cents and still took three van loads to Goodwill.

Amount Raised: $3,000

One family specifically asked for only large items and kids' clothes. They took the nicest kids' clothes to the semiannual kids' consignment sale and made $200. The rest they put in the garage sale, priced at $1. They listed several large items on Craigslist before the garage sale, making $650 in advance.

Amount Raised: $2,000

The Oberhauser family advertised their two yard sales on the internet, in newspapers, and on Christian radio. Flyers described their adoption of their two-year-old son from Ukraine, and many shoppers made donations above their purchase amount.

Amount Raised: $4,000

Cash for Shoes

When you're sorting through garage sale leftovers, look for shoes you can use to kick-start this fund-raiser. It's another easy one that doesn't feel like you're asking, but rather helping. Does anyone ever get annoyed when someone volunteers to take your junk off their hands? I don't think so.

I found out about this program from a family doing a drive to help pay for medical bills. I contacted the organization, Cash4shooz, to see if the program would work for adoptive families and it does.

The shoes are processed and shipped to facilities that employ eighty-five local people in third-world countries where they are ultimately sold, again providing jobs and income for others as well as meeting a physical need. So not only are you raising funds but you're helping create jobs in other countries.

The price per pound of shoes fluctuates but, for example purposes, is currently about 60 cents per pound. (That jumps to 70 cents per pound if you collect over 3,000 pounds of shoes.) A pair of shoes weighs, on average, 1.5 pounds. So if your goal was to raise $10,000, you would need about 14,285 pounds of shoes, or roughly 9,500 pairs.

Now, that might sound like a lot, but this is a perfect fund-raiser for recruiting helpers to spread the word *wide*. A shoe drive can also be done over a long period of time if you can establish drop off stations at several local places like your kid's school, church, and local businesses.

Here are some tips that Cash4shooz gives:

- Make announcements at schools, church, local newspapers, radio, and so on. Provide drop-off locations.
- If you have other groups helping you, offer incentives. For example, if you're a school doing a drive, you could have a class competition and the class that collects the most shoes gets a pizza or ice cream party. If you have friends collecting for you, offer a restaurant gift card or something fun for whoever collects the most.
- Drop flyers (with your contact info) at your neighbors' homes offering to pick up unwanted shoes on a specific day.
- If you know other couples adopting, multiple groups can participate at the same time. Groups of shoes can be weighed separately to help divide the money.
- A fun way to get schools, churches, or a community to participate is to collect enough shoes to line up end to end for a mile.

Maybe from house to house in a neighborhood or around the school's field.

- Pulling in the media helps get the word out.
- Collect for at least four weeks, but you can actually do it for a lot longer. Or have a couple of big drives and wait until the end to have them picked up.

One family got their whole community involved and raised $28,000 for medical expenses.

Cash4shooz is located in Southern California but they can work with people from anywhere except San Diego. Your distance determines minimum weights that need to be met to make it cost-effective for freight. Inside southern California there is a 1,200 pound minimum (roughly forty-five full black lawn garbage bags). If you are outside southern California you have to pay freight charges which can range from $650 to $2,500. In order to make this worthwhile, they ask that you collect a minimum of 15,000 pounds. If you collect more than 15,000 pounds, Cash4shooz will cover 50 percent of the freight charges.

Cash4shooz also collects used clothing although the price per pound is much less, about 15 cents per pound. Visit cash4shooz.com to get a quote and for more information.

5k Fun Run / Walk

Nicole and Chris raised $5,000 with their 5k "Show Love Fun Run." The couple and six friends from church spent three months planning the event.

The 125 runners who participated paid a registration fee of $40 per person (or $80 per family), which included a T-shirt, on-course support, and snacks after the race.

Nicole and Chris advertised the Fun Run through community calendars, flyers around the planned run course, and posters at all the coffee shops within a five-mile radius. They also used Facebook,

Twitter, and their church bulletin to promote the event. Local running clubs were notified via active.com.

Run day included other activities for the two hundred people who attended—coffee and pastries, a photo booth, cotton candy, balloon artists, face painting, and a huge bounce house for the kids. Six local business sponsors covered the cost of these activities, as well as permits and event insurance.

A month before the run, the couple announced more than a dozen giveaway items and presold raffle tickets for $1. As word got out, they received additional donated raffle items and had more than thirty items by race day. They sold 2,100 raffle tickets, mostly on the day of the run.

The giveaways included an adoption quilt, handmade pottery, sports tickets, ski lift tickets, a massage, photography session, iPod Nano, autographed music CDs, gift certificates for jewelry, haircuts, auto detailing, restaurants, and more. The couple used traveler points to get the two iPods, but everything else was donated.

Nicole said next time she would use the more expensive items, like the iPods, in a silent auction instead of including them in the giveaway.

Not only did the fun run raise money, but the couple educated others about adoption by setting up an information table and placing various orphan and adoption facts along the course. Two families who attended are now considering adoption.

The 5k was so much fun that Nicole and Chris plan to make it a yearly event and use the money to help other adopting families. They said they will target more running clubs, possibly even offering them a discount on registration. Since the park where the run was held allowed pets on leashes, they plan to do a better job of advertising at pet stores, groomers, and kennels.

A survey at the Fun Run showed them that word of mouth accounted for more than half of the attendance.

Amount Raised: $5,000

Movie Night and Silent Auction

The Boulton family held a movie night and silent auction fundraiser at their church to help fund their adoption of a toddler from Ethiopia.

They showed a family-friendly movie on a large screen in the church gym and asked for a $10 donation per family. About twenty families attended and brought their own camp chairs and blankets.

Friends got involved and organized a corresponding bake sale and silent auction. The bake sale coordinator made sure that the donated cakes and cookies covered a variety of flavors and arranged everything during the sale. Church small groups and friends donated themed baskets, goods, and services for the silent auction. The auction included a wide range of items so that even those who couldn't spend a lot could still find something on which to bid.

Auction items included movie-themed baskets, handmade items, gift cards, a "date night" basket, and tickets to a Lakers game and an NFL game. One friend created a "Trunk of Love" full of clothes and items for the Boultons' soon-to-be adopted daughter. The winner gave the trunk to the Boultons as a gift. The trunk sold for $150.

The Boultons advertised the event on their blog and with flyers.

Amount Raised: $3,000

Note: Please be aware of copyright issues for these types of events. Even if you don't charge admission and instead ask for a "suggested donation," public viewing of a film requires special permission. You will need to obtain permission from either the copyright holder, the distributor, or one of the film industry licensing companies. Many times if you let them know it is a one-time event to raise money for charity, they will give you permission. Do a Google search for "public performance rights movies" for more information.

Both Hands Widow/Orphan Project

Several times the Bible lists orphans and widows together and commands us to care for them both. The Both Hands Foundation (bothhands.org) creates a way for you to do just that—care for a widow and fund-raise for the adoption of an orphan.

Both Hands does require a grant application and approval through Lifesong for Orphans. However, founder J. T. Olson says that every family who applies has been approved for the project.[1]

Years ago, Olson asked a friend to sponsor him in a golf tournament to raise funds for women in crisis pregnancies. The friend wrote back and said he'd gladly support his efforts if J. T. was working on a widow's house instead of playing golf.

Five years later, another friend of J. T.'s was adopting four children from Moldova and needed to raise funds for their expenses. J. T. remembered the letter, and the idea for Both Hands was born.

Once approved for a Both Hands/Lifesong grant, adoptive families recruit volunteers to help them for a one-day work project on the home of a widow. A minimum of ten volunteers is needed, but the more you have, the better. Diversify the age of your team; it helps with fund-raising as well as on work day.

Each volunteer, along with the adoptive family, sends out a fund-raising letter to their circle of friends and family, explaining the project and a bit about the adoption. Families who get a total of six hundred letters sent out usually raise a minimum of $10,000 according to Olson.[2] That seems like a lot of letters but if you have a team of twenty people that's only thirty letters each.

Also, have your team check to see if matching donations are available from their employer for what they raise.

Next, the adoptive family partners with a widow who needs help around her home. Local churches and community service organizations like Meals on Wheels can help you find someone to help if you don't know anyone. Do a video interview with the widow you'll be helping at the beginning of the process. It will help you cast vision and motivate your volunteers.

Try to find work that is more labor-intensive than materials-intensive—things like paint, landscape cleanup, cleaning, and minor repairs won't require much cost. Once you determine the type of work your team will be doing, contact local businesses and ask if they will donate supplies. Paint is one of the easiest things to get donated but families have had lumber and roofing supplies donated before.

Both Hands has a fantastic staff that walks you through every step of the process and answers any questions you have. They suggest at least a ten- to twelve-week lead time for your project.

On work day, have fun and enjoy the opportunity to encourage the woman you're helping. Both Hands is sure to be a life-changing experience for everyone involved.

Stacey and Rodney Kennedy gathered forty volunteers, including several contractors who donated their time, and went to work on a hot Nashville summer day. Wendy, the widow they were serving, lost her husband to cancer at the age of thirty-one, and is now raising their young son, Quinn, on her own.

The Kennedy crew tackled six projects for Wendy:

- Washed, detailed, and vacuumed Wendy's car (a perfect job for some of the older kids)
- Painted the porch trim and front siding
- Repainted the mailbox and cleaned up the flowerbed
- Tore out overgrown bushes in backyard and trimmed bushes in front yard
- Moved the compost bin and wood pile to a better location
- Tore down and rebuilt the rickety back deck (They tore it down on the project day and a contractor donated his time to come back and build the new deck on a different day. Home Depot donated all the lumber.)

They also trimmed the bushes and landscaping of the widow across the street.

After their experience, Stacey advises families to have an army of people praying for you at all times. She said the spiritual warfare on them individually and on their marriage was intense from the moment they filled out the application to Lifesong. They knew God had called them to do it, but she said it was ten times harder, emotionally and spiritually, then getting their home study approved.

The Kennedys' Both Hands project brought $10,250 into their adoption fund. They benefited from the matching donations of several of the volunteers' employers. Stacey said,

> What a privilege to be able to give a day of service to our dear friend Wendy, a young widow and her son Quinn...AND the widow across the street! This Saturday, surrounded by our friends and many that we just met, devoting the day to hard labor in the intense summer heat, we experienced the Gospel of Jesus being lived out before our eyes. To bring home an orphan into our family by serving two widows is truly one of the highlights of our entire lives. We are so incredibly grateful and blessed.

Amount Raised: $1,000–$27,000 (average of $10,000)

Dinner

When you hear "benefit dinner," don't be intimidated. It doesn't have to be a black tie affair with prime rib.

Think about your circle of friends and family and gear your dinner toward them. If you're a casual, laid-back bunch, do a BBQ or spaghetti dinner. One of my friends cooked up a soup and bread night. She asked a bunch of her friends to cook different kinds of soup in slow cookers. They bought bread, bowls, and spoons and charged $5 per person. Donated baked goods were sold for dessert. At the end of the night, they netted $5,000!

If your connections are used to black tie dinners and willing to pay a higher ticket price, then by all means, go for a more formal event.

Either way, a dinner will take some time to organize; so give yourself at least two to three months to prepare. A dinner event is the perfect time to hold a silent auction, which means you may want even more planning time.

Here are some things to consider as you're planning:

Volunteers—You'll need people to help advertise, collect money, cook, serve, sell desserts, and clean up. If you are including a silent auction, you'll need a set of several volunteers to work on collecting donations and organizing them.

Location—Ideally, find a location you can use for free. It could be someone's backyard, a church or school multipurpose room, or an event hall. Make sure it has a nearby kitchen you can use.

Food—Whether you choose to do it yourself with your volunteer team or have it catered, it never hurts to ask for donated items. As an alternative, you might find a few local businesses that are willing to sponsor the event. In exchange for some money to cover your costs, you can advertise for the business throughout the event. Drinks can be as simple as tea and lemonade. Instead of including dessert, consider getting friends to donate baked goods and sell them.

Program—Plan to have a program, even if it is brief. Take the time to share the story of why you are adopting and why you're raising funds. There are lots of great videos on the general topic of orphans that you could show. Again, depending on the crowd, you might include music or a guest speaker.

Price—Set your price according to the style of your event. Consider offering a "per family" price as well as an individual cost. This will encourage young families who have children and don't want to pay for a babysitter. Make a way for people to donate at a later point in the evening—a jar or basket by the dessert table, for example. You could even do something fun like a money tree.

Activities—As you read through this book, you may see other things, besides a silent auction, that would pair well with the dinner—movie night, karaoke, or family pictures. If you are selling T-shirts, jewelry, or coffee, put that out on a table. Depending on the location, see if you can get a bounce house donated or sponsored. Having kids occupied will free up their parents to look at auction items. (Find a teenager who can act as supervisor for the bounce house and limit how many children are inside at a time.)

Giveaways—Have a few fun giveaways during the night. Even if you're not doing a silent auction, see if friends or business will donate a few items—gift cards or certificates are perfect. Include a couple of your adoption T-shirts. You can manage the giveaways through a raffle ticket system (give each person a ticket as they pay) or do something like put numbers under the chairs. (See chapter 15 for more information about the legalities of giveaways.)

Advertising—Use every method you can think of. An invitation website makes e-mail invitations and RSVPs easy. Set up an event on your Facebook page and invite all your friends. Ask them to share it with others they know. Promote it on your blog. Ask if you can place an announcement in the church bulletin or put up flyers. Ask to send a flyer home with the other students in your child's class.

Whatever you do, *don't* try to do it all yourself. Enlist all those people who have asked, "What can I do to help?"

Amount Raised: $1,000–$10,000

Stephen and Dottie Story organized a catered banquet and asked invitees to choose the level of donation they wanted to give. Dan Cruver, director of Together for Adoption, spoke to the seventy-five people in attendance about God's heart for adoption. (The Story family gave Dan an honorarium and covered his travel expenses.)

Amount Raised: $10,000

Pancake Breakfast

Jillian and John's pancake breakfast brought over $4,400 into their adoption fund. Held in their church fellowship hall, the breakfast included pancakes, eggs, bacon, juice, coffee, and tea. The bacon and eggs were donated by farmers from the church, leaving the Burdens to only buy pancake ingredients and the drinks. Even though the cost was only marginally cheaper, the Burdens decided to make the pancakes from scratch and got rave reviews from the crowd.

They bought their ingredients at a restaurant supply store open to the public, which allowed them to return unopened bags of flour and cartons of syrup. They returned $100 worth of food at the end, but were glad they had extra rather than not enough.

They also spent a little over $30 on some mason jars and flowers for simple table decorations.

Jillian and John wanted to be sure all their friends and family could participate so they advertised a suggested donation of $10 per person or $30 per family. Most people gave far more than that amount. Total attendance was just over one hundred people.

Fortunately their friends and small group stepped up to help. Six adults set up the tables and main serving station the night before the breakfast. Jillian and John premixed dry ingredients for pancakes and got all the cooking stations prepared the night before as well.

At the breakfast they had two adults at the donation table, seven adults cooking, two adults washing dishes, three teenagers running food to the serving line, two adults serving food (Jillian and John so they could say hello to everyone), two adults at the drink station, two adults selling T-shirts and jewelry, and one adult babysitting all the volunteers' kids—twenty-two people all together.

They offered their adoption T-shirts and jewelry for sale at the breakfast, but did not count those sales toward the final tally.

Jillian advises others to plan your timeline and then start cooking twenty minutes earlier than you think you should. Give your volunteers clear, written instructions. Estimate how much food you should make and add 20 percent.

As far as advertising the event, the big push began a month before when they created a Facebook event. Two weeks before the event they talked it up on their Facebook accounts and blogs, including taking photos of them shopping for ingredients. They also posted the event to the church's Facebook page.

Amount Raised: $4,500

Silent Auction

A silent auction is the perfect fund-raiser to pair with another event like a benefit concert, dinner, or movie night. It can also be done online, which is explained later in the chapter.

Start soliciting donations a minimum of two to three months in advance. This is a great opportunity to use friends who have offered their time. (If they haven't offered, then ask anyway.) Put them to work getting donations for the auction.

Items can be goods or services and can come from companies, individuals, or groups. Donations might be single items or a themed basket of goods.

If you belong to a church with small groups, ask if you can contact the leaders and ask if their group would put together a themed basket of goodies. This lets people help without a big expense. After you collect their basket, use shrink wrap or colored cellophane and some ribbon to package it nicely.

When soliciting for large items like electronics and appliances, you may have better responses with independently run stores. Instead of an outright donation, some might agree to give you the item at cost and not charge you until after the auction. (Make the minimum bid on the item equal to your cost.)

Make a master list of all the items collected for the auction; include the donor's name, his or her contact information, and any cost to you. Include space to note who won the item, final price, and if he or she has paid.

Recruit volunteers to help as judges, bankers, and runners.

Auction Details

Using a small label, number each item to correspond with your master list.

Print a bid sheet for each item that details the item, its number, how much it is worth, and who donated it. Include a minimum bid (approximately 25 percent of the retail value) and the minimum bid increment. A good guideline is: $1 for items up to $50, $2 if the item is worth $50 to $100 and $5 for items over $100. Add several lines with columns for the bidder's name, phone number, and his or her bid amount.

If needed, make up a certificate for donated services that don't have a premade certificate. For small items like event tickets, you may want to print a certificate instead of displaying the actual tickets to prevent them from getting lost.

Place judges near the tables to ensure that bids are meeting the right increases, to answer questions, and to monitor the donations. Have extra blank bid sheets available in case the first bid sheet fills up.

Tape the bid sheets down to the table in front of the item and secure a pen on a string near each sheet.

Give people a warning when there are only ten or fifteen minutes left to bid. If there are items with no bids, be sure to promote those.

When the time is up, have the judges immediately pick up the bid sheets. Double check them to be sure the bidding increased correctly.

Have the bankers sort the bid sheets by last name of the winner. If someone won multiple items, staple those sheets together and total the amount they owe.

Call auction winners to the bank table one or two at a time to pay for their items. While they are paying, have a runner go get the item from the tables. (If for some reason a winner does not want to pay for the item he or she won, move on to the next highest bidder.)

Not all winners will still be at the event; that is why you collected phone numbers. In the day or two after the auction, call winners and arrange for payment and pickup of their item. (If there are a lot of leftover items, ask one or two of your volunteers to help you make calls and get items delivered.) Follow up with thank-you notes to your donors and volunteers.

Amount Raised: $1,000–$5,000 or more

Examples of Auction Items

Goods
   Event tickets—sports, theater, ballet
   Memberships—fitness center, museum

Trip/vacation packages or timeshare stays
Electronics—computers, DVD players, iPod, video game players
Appliances and furniture

Services
  Photography session
  Website design services
  Tax preparation
  Lessons—music, swimming, karate
  Auto—oil change, tire rotation and balance, detailing
  Birthday party packages—pizza parlors, kid gyms
  Dental—teeth whitening
  Home services—pest control, landscaping, pool care, painting, furnace/AC servicing
  Spa/pampering—hair styling, manicure/pedicure, massage, spa treatments

Themed Basket Ideas
  Movie Night—DVDs, popcorn, candy, drinks, gift card to video rental store
  Date Night—restaurant or movie theater gift cards, candles, romantic music CD
  Gourmet Kitchen—spices, gadgets, cookbook
  Family Fun Night—board games, puzzles, DVDs, candy, music
  Wii (or other console)—extra remotes, video games, snacks, gaming guides
  Coffee—flavored coffee, coffee cups, travel mugs, gift card to coffee shop
  Baking—cookie cutters, pot holders, cookbooks, measuring cups, cookie mixes, frosting, sprinkles
  Pool Party—pool toys, sunscreen, beach towels, goggles
  Ice Cream—toppings, bowls, scoops, gift card to ice cream parlor
  Christmas—ornaments, wrapping paper, cards, decorations
  Disney—toys, games, movies

Gardening—hand shovel, seeds, bulbs, watering can, hat, pots, gift card to garden center

Do-It-Yourself—tools, how-to books, gift card to hardware store

Spa—bath products, tub pillow, music CD, gift card for massage or pedicure

Sports—game tickets, jersey, ball, hats, T-shirt

Books (adult or child)—books, reading light, gift card to bookstore

Chocolate Lovers—candy, gourmet chocolate, hot chocolate mix, gift card to candy shop

Golf—balls, bag tag, towels, tees, golf gloves, gift card for eighteen holes

Babies—bibs, bottles, Onesies, pacifiers, blankets, rattles, soft books

Grill Master—BBQ tools, sauces, cookbooks, apron

Camping—lantern, tin dish sets, hiking guides, trail mix, compass, pocket knife

Car Care—auto wax, cleaners, tire gauge, car care books, steering wheel cover, chamois, sun shade

Hobby Related—scrapbooking, sewing, model cars, jewelry making

Karaoke Night

Kenny and Catherine Besk raised over $20,000 for their adoption with several different fund-raisers, one of which is destined to provide lots of laughter along with donations.

A local family pub and grille in Santa Cruz agreed to donate space for the Besks to host a karaoke night. The karaoke service was offered at half price, and the pub owner offered to cover that cost as well.

Here's how karaoke night works:

- For $10 a person signs up a friend to sing and picks the song they have to sing.
- When the friend's name is called, he or she can pay $5 to change the song or add a friend to sing with.

- Or for $15, he or she can get out of singing the song, and the person who signed him or her up has to sing it.
- Those who pay $30 when they arrive can get in, cheer and laugh, but are safe from having to sing all night.

With a fun group of friends, karaoke night is bound to be a blast! **Amount Raised: $1,300**

Michael and Heidi raised $1,700 with their karaoke night, which they held at their church. Several people out of state donated to have people sing.

Want to take it a step further and have some tech know-how? Find out who is coming to your karaoke night. Then post on their Facebook walls that they'll be participating in your fund-raiser and offer online sign-ups for a premium price. If his or her college buddy wants to see and hear a rousing rendition of "Living on a Prayer," he or she donates $25 (or more) for a virtual sign up. You videotape the performance and post the item on their Facebook wall. For time constraints you could probably only take a limited number of virtual sign-ups but it's a fun way to spread your story.

Concert

Benefit concerts are a great fund-raising idea if you're connected with musicians and can put some time and energy into advertising. Combine a concert with a silent auction and sales of T-shirts or other similar items to maximize the opportunity.

If you attend church, ask your worship team if they would host a "Night of Worship" to benefit your adoption. Take ten minutes to share about the need of orphans and specifically your adoption journey. Whether you sell tickets or ask for donations at the door, make a way for people to give additional donations.

The Besk family took advantage of their art-centered community and talented friends by putting on a benefit concert. Two local bands, Dangle Root and Hurricane Roses, donated their time and one of the band members got the concert space donated. There was a suggested $10 donation at the door, and the Besks sold original concert posters painted by a friend.

Amount Raised: $1,800

Restaurant Fund-Raisers

Many restaurants offer fund-raising nights for nonprofit organizations. If you are working with a 501(c)(3) grant organization (see page 97), you can use the following idea as well, with the funds going into your grant.

Restaurant fund-raisers take very little work other than contacting the restaurant and advertising the event. Many chain restaurants offer fund-raising nights, but each individual owner may operate differently. Some require your friends to bring in a preprinted flyer when they dine; some just have customers tell the wait staff they came to support you. Fund-raising nights are usually held on one of the least-busy weekday nights, and you receive a percentage of the sales from your referrals.

Many major chain restaurants offer fundraisers (just search online), but many locally owned restaurants host fund-raiser nights as well and may offer you a bigger percentage. When you contact a restaurant, here are some questions to ask:

What percentage will our group receive? (Usually between 10 to 25 percent.)

What days are available?

What hours are available?

Is it limited to just our referrals or will we receive a percentage from everyone who dines during the time period?

Do takeout or drive-thru orders count?

Can we set up an informational display and solicit general donations during the night? (If so, be sure the display features your nonprofit grant organization and adds your personal story.)

You can raise anywhere from a few hundred dollars to over $1,000, but the good thing about restaurant fund-raisers is that you can schedule several of them throughout your adoption process.

Amount Raised: $200–$1,000 or more

Zumba Fitness Party

While not the biggest money raiser, Catherine Besk says their Zumba Fitness Fund-Raiser was one of her favorites. Zumba, one of the newest exercise trends, uses Latin-inspired dance in a fun, high-energy fitness program. One of Catherine's friends, who is an instructor, donated her time and got her studio to agree to let them use the space for free. People paid $15 for the one-hour Zumba class and had a ton of fun.

Amount Raised: $275

The McKinney family worked like crazy to fund-raise the $25,000 they needed to adopt a little girl from Ethiopia. Their Zumba party was a *big* success! They started out with one instructor who then recruited two more friends so they could offer two forty-five-minute Zumba sessions. They presold tickets (minimum donation of $10) through an invitation website and printed tickets that they gave their friends to sell. They even gave their friends some incentive and offered $100 cash prize to the person who sold the most tickets. (The winner ended up donating it back to the adoption fund.) They created a fun photo booth, played adoption videos, offered snacks, and had a raffle drawing as well.

Amount Raised: $3,000

Thinking Out of the Box

There is no idea too crazy right? Think you'd be willing to shave your head?

Kevin Hendricks decided it was definitely worth it when he and his wife, Abby, were adopting their son Milo from Ethiopia. With hair down to his shoulders, he pledged to shave his head if he could raise

$2,000 by his birthday. He mailed out letters to 250 of their friends to explain the idea and tell them about their adoption. Kevin included a FAQ sheet answering common adoption questions and explained why they needed to raise money.

On a full-color business card, he put a picture of himself with long hair on one side, and a Photoshopped picture of himself bald on the other side.

In the two months leading up to his birthday, forty-five people donated to the project. On his birthday, Kevin videotaped the shaving, photographed his newly shiny head, and sent the picture, along with a thank-you note, to each of the donors.

His "hairbrained" idea didn't seem so crazy when they added $4,500 to their adoption fund!

Kevin attributes the success to the amount of time and effort he spent crafting the letter and including the pictures. They chose not to use the Internet for the project because of their adoption agencies advice about online fund-raising.

Kevin had so much fun with the idea that he's done some additional hair-related fund-raisers to raise money for clean water through Charity: Water.

Amount Raised: $4,500

Blessed by Friends

One of the things I love hearing about is the way friends and family rally around adoptive families, sometimes coming up with and implementing amazing fund-raisers all on their own.

Sarah and Steve Carter were blown away when two of their engaged friends asked wedding guests to give toward the Carter's adoption in lieu of gifts. The couple made a beautiful video that shared their heart and then allowed Sarah and Steve to share about their Ghana adoption journey. They sent the DVD to all their wedding guests along with a RSVP/Donation card. (Guests could also give at the wedding.) Two months after their wedding, the couple presented the Carters with a check for $7,000—a third of their needed adoption funds.

Amount Raised $7,000

A couple of months before they were scheduled to head to Uganda to pick up their new son, Lara Dinsmore's blog was lovingly hijacked by two of her friends who threw her a virtual baby shower. With the goal of funding the Dinsmores' plane tickets, they had gathered some great door prizes including a Canon EOS Rebel T3i camera, T-shirts, and gift certificates. They set a goal of raising $5,000 in a week and they did it!

Amount Raised: $5,000

More Ideas

Bingo—Bingo supplies are available at your local party store. Get some prizes donated and have a fun night with friends.

Bowling Tournament—Ask a local bowling alley to donate or give you a reduced price on lanes on a less busy night. Charge a registration fee for teams of four bowlers. Offer a great prize, preferably donated, to the winning team.

Car Wash—Put your kids to work, get their friends or your church youth group involved. Ask for donations.

Dance-a-thon—Pick a theme (50s, disco, and so on) and charge an entry fee. Find a DJ who will donate his or her time and get local businesses to sponsor prizes for Best Costume and Best Dance Moves. Sell baked goods. As an alternative, participants could gather pledges for each half hour they dance and see who can dance the longest.

Skate-a-thon—Same as the dance-a-thon but hold it at the local ice skating or roller skating rink.

Golf Tournament—Work with a local golf course to coordinate a benefit golf tournament. Charge a per team entry fee. Ask local businesses to sponsor prizes or investigate "hole-in-one" prize insurance.

CHAPTER FOURTEEN
SALES-DRIVEN FUND-RAISERS

Seems that everyone who is adopting is selling something. Why? Because it works and there are dozens of ideas. You're only limited by your creativity and your time. Even more than most fund-raisers, your sales are going to directly reflect the amount of time and energy you put into it. Some of these ideas have a wide potential income range because you can either take the laid-back approach or go full gusto. You'll see what I mean when you read some of the stories.

Handmade Items

First, look at your existing talents. Do you paint? scrapbook? woodwork? make jewelry? sew? quilt? Hundreds of adoptive families are earning money for their adoptions by using their existing creative talents. There are several avenues that can be used to sell handmade items: eBay, your own blog, Facebook, Etsy, and so on.

Before a referral of a girl from Colombia, one waiting aunt decided to put her sewing skills to work and take advantage of her stash of fabric remnants to create "Bags for ZaZa" to help bring her niece home. Several others joined the sewing circle to create fun, funky messenger bags and sell them online.

They placed ads on Craigslist and contacted local upholstery shops to solicit leftover fabric and materials. This helped keep costs low as the bulk of their materials were donated.

They sold the bags online using a blog and a silent auction format. They listed each bag with several photos and a starting price of $25. People bid on the bag by writing their bid in the comments section. The average sales price was $40 with one bag selling for $150. Buyers then paid actual shipping costs.

"ZaZa" came home from Colombia in December 2010.

Amount Raised: $6,900

While waiting for their referral from Ethiopia, Debi came up with the idea to make wooden Africa-shaped Christmas ornaments. Her dad is a woodworker and volunteered a lot of his time. He cut, Debi sanded, and then she brought the ornaments home to paint and embellish. She's since started doing the woodwork herself. Debi sold several hundred ornaments to people all over the United States and Canada. Now she also makes magnets, key chains, wall hangings, and more.

Amount Raised: $2,000

Hilary Helms's handmade sign business, Philosophy Designs, actually started in an effort to pay off medical bills incurred when their son, Jude, was sick and hospitalized. Using free fence wood collected from people replacing their fences, Hilary's hand-painted signs featuring everything from scripture verses and family rules to favorite sports teams.

"God provided and made it way bigger than I had imagined," Hilary said. During their adoption of Isaac from Ethiopia she auctioned several signs specifically for those costs. She also donated two signs every month to other adoptive family auctions, some of which brought in as much as $500. The Helms family did a special auction with several signs to raise money for their airfare and brought in $1,750, but all together Hilary estimates her sign business brought in almost $10,000 in a year.

Amount Raised: $10,000

T-Shirts and Wearables

T-shirts seem to be the most popular item for adoptive families to sell, and there are some terrific designs out there. Some people have raised a few hundred dollars and others have raised thousands.

You can do T-shirt sales three ways depending on how much time and resources you have to devote. First, you can come up with a completely original design, find a screen printer, take orders, and handle the mailing. Second, you can purchase predesigned artwork and use that company's recommend screen printer. Or you can use one of the companies with predesigned shirts, take preorders, and buy from them in bulk. Each way has its own advantages.

If you're doing shirt sales all on your own, a few pieces of advice:

- Have a professional help with the artwork. If you don't have a friend who is a designer, ask the screen printing company. Most of them have designers on staff who can help take your vision and make it look good. Be sure you are happy with the design before you give them the final OK. A good design is everything! I, and other adoptive parents, often buy T-shirts if I like the design. Most of the time I don't even know the adopting family.
- Take preorders. You don't want to have hundreds of unsold shirts taking up room in your garage and eating up your adoption savings. The screen printer can provide you with a digital mockup of the design on a shirt that you can post online. You can also have them print up a small quantity of shirts (minimum order might be twelve) to start wearing around and show people the quality of the shirt. You'll pay more per shirt for your sample pieces, but it's worth the comfort knowing you won't have a ton of leftover stock.
- Choose a quality shirt. I confess that over the years of designing T-shirts I've become a bit of a shirt snob. I would happily pay a few bucks extra to get a nice soft, fitted T-shirt rather than a cheap, thick boxy tee. I know I'll wear it more. American Apparel, Next Level Apparel, Anvil, Alternative Apparel all

have really nice shirts. Consider the shirt weight. Anything below 5.0 oz will start to get a little transparent. Make sure to find out if the material is preshrunk. Some of these brands may run a bit small, especially if you select a more fitted shirt, so you will want to warn people and possibly have a few samples for them to look at. Your screen printer should also be able to provide you with sizing charts for the T-shirts you select.

• Go broader than just adoption. I've seen some super cute shirts that say "Adoption Rocks" or "Adopt One. Change One" but not everyone wants to be a walking billboard for adoption. If you broaden your theme to hope, mercy, love, change, or even to the country you're adopting from, you'll have a much wider audience. I probably have half a dozen T-shirts with an Africa theme that I've bought from other families that don't specifically mention adoption. I designed "Love Crosses Oceans" shirts and artwork for my brother's adoption fund-raiser and people have bought them because they were passionate about missions or the countries we used. One of my favorite T-shirts simply says "Every Heart Deserves a Home."

Bryce and Leanne Boddie of Texas raised approximately $2,500 with their adoption T-shirts. They gave shirts to all their immediate family and wore the shirts to church a lot to help spread the word. The Boddies also used the same design on reusable grocery bags, raising another $500 (approximately $5 to $10 profit per bag). They found that the bags also helped build awareness about international adoption.

Amount Raised: $3,000

147 Million Orphans

147 Million Orphans' broad product line of T-shirts, jewelry, bags, and hats is available to adoptive families for fund-raising. They have two types of fund-raising programs. You can do one or both.

The "Bulk Order Program" allows the family to take preorders and then buy the products at a bulk discount and distribute to buyers. Their Adoption Fund-Raising Family Kit ($100) provides samples of several items to help pre-sell the products. You can set the price of each item at the retail price or charge slightly more to increase your profits. This program allows you a higher profit, complete control over the selling process, and payment is made directly to you. The Bulk Order Program includes twenty-four of their catalog items.

The "Partnership Program" gives you a unique link to the website 147millionorphans.com and all sales from that link give you a 30 percent commission (excluding tax and shipping). Payments are mailed quarterly and only directly to your agency. All shipping is handled by 147 Million Orphans, and this allows you to sell all forty of their catalog items.

The Ugandan paper bead necklaces are the most popular item. Made by women in Uganda who roll the beads from recycled paper, the beads are dipped in varnish and threaded onto string. (Prior to learning how to bead, most of the women picked trash or turned to prostitution to provide for their children.)

Families can sell 147 Million Orphan products for a twelve-month period as long as they are still in the process of adopting. Participating families have earned from $500 to $10,000 for their adoptions.

Adoption Tees

Started by adoptive parents Russ and Ginger Moore, adoption tees.com merchandise is centered around the idea that "One Changes Everything," a message that came up over and over even before they committed to adoption. Adoption Tees products are graphically appealing and take a lot of the work out of your hands. Adoptive families start by ordering one of the starter kits (priced from $30 to $90) to give you samples to show people while you take preorders. When you are ready, purchase your items from Adoption Tees at a

30 percent discount and put your profits into your adoption fund. Adoption Tees will also do custom screen printing.

Show Hope

Show Hope offers their shirts to adoptive families at wholesale prices. They provide presale order forms to approved families. You pre-sell shirts for $25 and order them from Show Hope at the wholesale rate of $15. See the website for information on minimum quantities (showhope.org).

Adoption Bug

Adoption Bug offers a 25 to 45 percent commission (varies by design) to adoptive families who can choose up to six of their designs to sell. You can also submit up to two original art designs. Adoption Bug prints and ships the shirts for you. Adoptive families simply submit the sign-up form, make their product selections, include a photo and a very brief bio, and Adoption Bug creates a dedicated online store they can use to advertise to friends and family. There are no start-up or out-of-pocket costs (adoptionbug.com).

Chrome Buffalo

Chrome Buffalo's tagline is "Fund-Raising Fueled by Fashion" and they hit the mark with top-quality designs that can be used by anyone wanting to fund-raise. They work a little differently in that each quarter (January, April, July, and October) the designers at Chrome Buffalo come up with four new T-shirt designs. You pick which design you'd like to sell and set up your ten-day "Drive" or campaign. While not adoption specific, there is usually at least one design that fits well for an adoption fund-raiser. One quarter they had a shirt that said "Hope Changes Everything." Other designs have included "Hope is my Anchor" and "Live Love." Personally, I think the broader theme works even better.

The T-shirts sell for $22 plus shipping. For every T-shirt sold during your ten-day drive, you earn $11. That's a great return considering

Chrome Buffalo does all the work other than spreading the word. At the end of your ten-day drive, Chrome Buffalo ships out your orders and sends you your money. No risk whatsoever. You can only run one fund-raising drive at a time, but you can come back and do it more than once, which means you can offer different T-shirt designs (Chromebuffalo.com).

Photography

As you share your adoption story, keep your ears open for offers of help from people who might have a skill you can use to raise funds. Photography is a perfect example. If you know someone who is a photographer, ask if he or she would donate some time to raise funds for your adoption. There are several ways you could organize a photography event. Also check with local retailers. The ones that have portrait studios often have fund-raising cards.

Portraits in the Park

Many photographers use a "portraits in the park" idea where they pick a picturesque location and book twenty- to thirty-minute sessions for family pictures, shooting eight or more different families in an afternoon. Set a suggested donation price for the portrait session and give each family a set number of high-resolution images on CD that they can take to any photo center for printing. This is a perfect thing to do in November when people want a nice family photo for their holiday cards.

Amount Raised: $250–$500

Studio-Style Portraits

If you have an indoor location that is suitable for setting up studio-style portrait sessions, schedule a family portrait day. Find a photographer willing to set up in your church or community center. Pre-sell portrait certificates for $20 that include the sitting fee and one free 8 x 10 portrait. The photographer will, of course, take multiple shots and allow the family to purchase additional photos. That's their incentive for offering their services to you and giving away the free 8 x 10. You keep the $20 session fee and they make money from selling additional portraits.

Russ and Katie Mohr are good friends with two photographers in St. Louis. When they heard about the Mohr's second adoption, the photographers stepped forward to help raise funds. When they organized a day of mini-sessions for high-end kids portraits, they had twenty slots offered at a discounted price of $200, even sponsoring two slots and allowing people to nominate deserving families. A friend in commercial real estate development donated space in one of his venues. The Mohrs supplied backdrops and food for the five volunteers who helped that day. Each family received a disc of high-resolution images from their shoot.

Amount Raised $5,000

Lori used her own skills as a photographer to raise money for their adoption, organizing a family holiday portrait session at a local bookstore. She asked for a suggested donation of $20 for which the family received a free 5 x 7. Families could also order a larger package and/or photo Christmas cards, allowing Lori to make even more money. Lori got the local photo lab to give her a discount on printing, which increased her profit. The bookstore agreed to serve as the pickup location. Lori advertised the event online, in the local newspapers, and with flyers.

Amount Raised: $2,000

Recycle and Resell

The Morgan family collected aluminum cans and foil for over a year. Friends and family (and *their* friends and family) joined the efforts, including a few hair salons that donated the foil they used to color hair. Twice the Morgans had "Can Our Yard" days where people dumped their aluminum collection on the Morgans' front lawn. The Morgans also hit the local college campus on game day and picked up cans. "The students may not realize at the time they are supporting us, but we took their cans anyway. We get a lot of strange looks, but we just chalk it up to being passionate about what God has called us to do!" they said. Whenever the Morgans collected a truckload full of cans, they'd make a trip to the local recycling center.

Amount Raised to Date: $3,000

Along with a garage sale, another family held a used media drive. They e-mailed local friends and asked for any unwanted books, movies, video games, music CDs, curriculum, and electronics.

Most of the items were sold on eBay. The items that didn't sell were taken took to a local media buyer; what they didn't buy was sold at the garage sale.

Amount Raised: $2,300

Luxury Linens

Sometimes a family's fund-raising journey is so successful it turns into an ongoing business.

Through a unique set of events, the Lancaster family received news that they could adopt the little girl from China whom they had been sponsoring through an orphan care ministry. But with five kids and one income, they didn't know where to find the $26,000 needed to bring Lori home.

A friend mentioned the idea of buying luxury bed linens at wholesale and reselling them, and that was the start of Lori's Linens. Sales started off fairly slow until the Lancasters' circle of friends began helping them sell the sheets.

In 2010, the company sold over 570 sets of Egyptian cotton sheets and helped the Lancasters bring Lori home. Now they help other adoptive families.

Lori's Linens provides order forms, a color chart, and one sample set of sheets to use during sales. The cost to your family depends on how many orders you have, but ranges from $27 to $30 per set. Using Lori's Linens suggested retail price ($45), each set provides an average profit of $15 to $18. Families can increase the sales price if they want. I bought a set from an adoptive family, and they're really soft and have held up well for the last two years.

Coffee

Your trips to Starbucks might be less frequent these days (if not, reread the chapter on trimming expenses), but you can use those coffee cravings to raise money.

Just Love Coffee, founded by adoptive parents, sells fair trade coffee and puts a portion of their profits into projects in Ethiopia. Their adoption fund-raising program offers you a customized order page where friends and family can purchase coffee. There is no up-front cost and all order fulfillment is handled by Just Love Coffee. You make $5 per bag and can continue selling for up to twelve months after your adoption is complete to help pay for post-placement costs. If you adopt a child with special needs who requires ongoing medical care, you can keep your store running indefinitely. Several other products, such as sampler packs and mugs, are available too and families make a percentage on those as well.

Adoptive families have raised $250,000 using Just Love Coffee. With some effort and marketing savvy, families have raised as much as $4,500.

Sarai and James Barnett are also Dave Ramsey fans and decided they wanted to raise the needed funds before they started their adoption. They set up a Just Love Coffee online page, but Sarai confesses she wasn't very good about blogging. But, she spent over forty hours a week working in a medical office building. And apparently doctor's offices live on coffee. She started selling at her office and then networked with other offices in the building by giving out some samples. Pretty soon she had a regular customer base hooked on the gourmet coffee. She also kept a variety of coffee on hand because people would come in her office looking for "the coffee lady." In a little over two years they had raised $4,500.

In addition to the Boddie family's online sales, they hosted a "coffee party." They ordered a couple of the sampler packs from Just Love

Coffee so friends could try them before placing orders. (They also sold their adoption T-shirts and reusable grocery bags at the event.) They raised $500 that night and sold about $200 in coffee.

Amount Raised: $150–$4,500

Jewelry and Handmade Items

Rebekah Blocher and her husband, Matt, create beautiful handmade ceramic jewelry for their company, Compelled Designs. With a heart for adoption and missions, they offer the pieces as fund-raisers for families and organizations. I love this fund-raiser because not only are the pieces gorgeous and practically sell themselves but also there is no risk!

When you order a fund-raising package Compelled Designs sends you a package of twenty necklaces. You sell them for the retail price of $24 (an easy price) using in-person sales, Facebook, your blog, or even at craft/vendor fairs. The only limitation is you can't sell them in an Etsy shop. When you've sold all twenty pieces, you pay Compelled Design $12 for each piece, keeping $12 for your adoption. That's $240 in profit for each set. At any time you can order additional pieces and you only pay for what you sell. If you have unsold pieces when you're done, simply send them back to Compelled Designs.

Delicate Fortress Creations products are not only gorgeous but are made by artisans all over the world. Working with twenty-five different organizations that fight human trafficking, illiteracy, poverty, modern slavery, and help at-risk children, DFC brings together a gorgeous selection of items.

One adoptive family recently made over $700 during their week-long fund-raiser. Some of these types of companies can tend to have high prices, but I was pleasantly surprised by the affordability of a lot of the Delicate Fortress Creations items.

DFC gives you 25 percent of all sales during your week-long fund-raiser. They handle marketing; you just forward the info to your friends and family. They track sales with a special coupon code, then send you a check.

Noonday Collection began in 2010 when Jessica Honegger started selling beautiful handmade goods made by Ugandan women to raise funds for their Rwanda adoption. Since then the company has grown and goods are sold online, through trunk shows, and through an Ambassador program.

You can host a trunk show and choose to receive a 10 percent reward in cash for your adoption fund. Or, if you're looking for a second income source you can become a Noonday ambassador.

Direct Sales

Pampered Chef, Tupperware, Avon, Gold Canyon Candles, Premier Designs—dozens of companies employ independent sales consultants to sell products through house parties and online catalog sales.

If you have a friend who is a consultant, ask if he or she would host a special party and donate the profits toward your adoption fund. There is also a list of consultants on my website who will do fund-raisers (juliegumm.com/book-extras/).

Better yet, gather several of these consultants right before the holidays for a special shopping event like Lara Dinsmore did with her "Stop 'N Shop for Adoption" in early November. One of Lara's friends is a successful direct sales consultant; so she used her work and contacts to help pull off the event. Each consultant that participated agreed to donate 50 percent of his or her commission to the Dinsmore's adoption fund. Lara's friend then followed up with each consultant after the event to collect the money.

Advertising for the Stop 'N Shop was done via Facebook, blogs, and flyers.

Amount Raised: $900

CHAPTER
FIFTEEN
SOCIAL MEDIA FUND-RAISING

Google "adoption blog" and you get over 24 million results—blogs chronicling adoptions from the foster care system, domestic private adoptions, and adoptions of kids from all over the world.

Having a blog is not only a great way to chronicle your journey and preserve it for your family history but also a great tool to raise awareness and funds. Even if you use Facebook and other social media avenues, you will probably find it helpful to have a blog. Some people will assume blogging will equal more time commitment, but a blog can be useful even if only updated a couple of times a month. It's a great "home base" for T-shirt sales, the long version of your adoption story, and information on other fund-raising efforts. Setting up a blog is free and easy with multiple platforms available.

Also, set up a PayPal account so you can receive donations toward your adoption. Setting up an account is easy and using PayPal's merchant services to add a "Donate Now" button to your blog or website makes collecting funds a breeze. (Money sent via PayPal designated as a "gift" doesn't incur any PayPal fees for the donor or the recipient. You keep 100 percent of the gift.) Link your PayPal account to a bank account at your bank and you can easily transfer money out of the PayPal account and into your savings. You may want to consider setting up a separate savings account for your adoption to help provide an added level of accountability. It will track where you are in relation to your goals. Make sure people are aware that donations to your fund via PayPal are not tax deductible for them.

If, later in your process, you partner with a grant organization that accepts donations on your behalf, you will likely still want a PayPal button for things like T-shirt sales and auctions.

Some people prefer the ease of paying from money they have in their own PayPal account and may prefer to donate that way even without the tax benefit.

During the fund-raising process, many families break up adoption costs into smaller sections and show a fund-raising thermometer to track their progress. For example, you might say, "We need $2,500 to complete our application and home study." Once that goal is met, celebrate, and then post the next goal, resetting your fund-raising thermometer. Smaller goals with quicker wins give you (and your donors) excitement and extra motivation as you continue toward the end goal.

Once you have the donation button set up, blog about your fund-raising efforts. A lot of people are unaware of the cost of adoption and are curious about how the money is used. Be up-front and honest with them and share from your heart just as you would in a fund-raising letter. Be sure to check with your agency regarding any limitations they might place on online fund-raising and blogging. Most agencies prohibit you from posting the real names or identifying photos of your children until after they are legally yours. We referred to Wendemagegn and Beza on our blog as W-boy and B-girl.

There are some specific fund-raisers that work well online, but first let's talk about using social media to receive direction donations.

The Direct Ask

If you are open to doing a direct ask, here are a few pointers.

Relay the need—This is the overall adoption finance picture, what you're doing to contribute, and a call for help.

Set a goal—Again, smaller goals are sometime more manageable and help create a sense of urgency. If you can tell your friends "We need $5,000 for our agency fee due in three weeks," then people have a deadline and an idea of how much their gift will help the overall picture.

Be persistent—You can't just ask once and never mention the need again. Keep people updated on progress made at least once every day or two. Say thank you online if appropriate. Obviously there is a balance to this. If you're posting to your Facebook status about your fund-raiser twelve times a day, your friends may grow tired.

Use multiple media—If you use Facebook and Twitter, take advantage of their reach. Ask friends and family to share your fund-raiser with their friends and family. You can create a fund-raising event on Facebook, but keep in mind that everyone you invite receives an e-mail notification each time you post to the event until they decline the event. Some may not realize how to get off the notification list, so you may want to send out a status early on telling them to decline the invite if they don't want any further notifications. Remember not everyone is on social media. Some people won't know about your fund-raising efforts unless you mail them a letter.

Create your own matching fund—If you have a few friends or family you think might be open to donating fairly sizable funds, approach them about donating toward a matching fund. When you have between $1,500 to $3,000, announce it as a matching fund and make a big drive to get other friends and family to donate, even in small amounts to meet the match.

Mary set up a birthday fund-raising event on Facebook with the goal of finding two hundred people to donate $100 toward their Uganda adoption in the three days before her birthday. Mary invited her friends and family who turned around and invited more people with just shy of 1,300 seeing the event. A couple of anonymous donors even agreed to match donations up to a certain amount. In that small window of time Mary raised $7,500.

Reward and Recognition

As people give general donations to your adoption fund, there are several ways to recognize them so that their investment in your journey is recorded for your child. What a powerful testimony to how much your child was loved even before he or she came to you.

Puzzle Pieces

Many families purchase a 250- to 500-piece puzzle and, as people make donations toward the fund, write the person's name on the back of a puzzle piece. You might choose to divide your total adoption costs by the number of pieces so that a fully assembled puzzle equals a fully funded adoption. Or you might choose to use the puzzle to meet a smaller goal.

Periodic updates on your blog can show how the puzzle is growing; the pieces with names are connected upside down. Let people know how many pieces are still available. When the puzzle is completed, you get to reveal the picture on the other side, which has been kept a surprise. The puzzle is then matted between two pieces of glass, framed, and hung in the adopted child's room.

Amount Raised: $2,500 or more

Quilt Pieces

The Halstead family gave people the opportunity to buy a fabric quilt square for $1 and then sign their name or encouraging message on the square. The squares, cut from donated fabric, were sold during a couple of fund-raising events and helped raise $2,500.

In the end, Jenna Halstead made one small quilt that she kept for the family, and she used the rest of the squares to make quilts for other children awaiting adoption. You could easily sell squares online as well and let people designate a message for their piece.

Amount Raised: $2,500

Painted Canvas

Five weeks before their court date, the Davis family still needed $10,000 to pay all their expenses. They bought a blank 24 x 30 canvas and divided it into 520 squares. Each square represented one $20 donation and the donor chose the color for the square. Using mostly social media to spread the word, the Davis family exceeded their goal. When they were finished they had a nice piece of abstract art to hang in their new child's room.

Amount Raised: $11,000

Tag the Bag

When the Johnson family was adopting their daughter, they created the "Tag the Bag" fund-raiser. They purchased a small used suitcase at a garage sale for $.50. Anyone donating to their daughter's adoption fund got their name written on the bag with a marker. They raised $3,500 and now use the bag to hold her keepsakes—things brought home from her native country and other childhood treasures as she grows. The family is using the same fund-raiser for their second adoption, and their son's bag is tagged with names of people who have donated a total of $7,500. Friends Catherine and Kenny Besk, used the idea for a shortened forty-eight-hour fund-raising drive to raise the cost of their airfare to Ethiopia. They received fifty-eight donations totaling $3,250.

Online Auctions

You can take the traditional silent auction and easily make an online variation where people use blog comments to bid on individual items. You can choose to host through your existing blog, but many find it easier to create a separate blog just for the auction and link to it from their main blog.

Just like a regular silent auction, allow yourself a few months to solicit donations. Refer to the silent auction list in chapter 14 for ideas of items that can be donated. The great part of an online auction is that you can reach a much bigger audience with items that don't have to be location specific. (If an item is location specific to your area, please be sure to note that in the item description.)

If possible, ask the people donating items to hang on to the item and mail it directly to the winner. You will want to have a photo of the item as well as a description, but hopefully those can be e-mailed to you. This will save you all the shipping costs.

Where do you get items for the auction? A lot of the same places you'd get them if you held a local auction. You might also reach out to Etsy shop owners or friends who make handmade things. I receive several inquires each month regarding items in my Etsy shop.

Other adoptive families might donate T-shirts or handmade items they made for their own fund-raisers.

On the auction blog, create one post listing each item donated. Make this post "sticky," meaning it always stays at the top of the front page of the blog. Depending on the blogging system you use, they may have a "sticky post" option, or you can just manually set the published date of the post to be earlier than all the other item posts. Then, each item up for auction will get its own post. Include a picture and as many details as possible. If the donor isn't covering shipping, you could add the shipping cost to the winning bid, just be sure to specify that in the item description. Finally, list the starting bid (half of retail value is generally a good starting point). To bid, people simply comment on the post with their bid amount. Depending on the value of the item you can specify increase amounts such as $5.

Halfway through the auction period, see if there are any items not attracting any bids, make sure to promote those on Facebook or on that sticky home page post.

When the auction time is done simply find the last blog comment and notify the winner. Ask him or her to submit payment via PayPal or by mailing a check. Forward their shipping information on to the item owner if necessary. If for some reason a bidder doesn't respond or pay, simply go to the bidder before him or her.

Jennifer and Trevor have two biological children and are adopting from Ethiopia. One of their most successful fund-raisers was an online auction, born out of Jennifer's passion for craft-oriented blogs.

Jennifer contacted craft bloggers she followed and friends who made handmade items, telling them about her family's adoption and the online auction. Some of the people she contacted also asked their readers for additional items. In the end, Jennifer had over eighty items including clothing, jewelry, baby items, and artwork.

Some of the donors sent the items to Jennifer. Others just e-mailed a picture and later mailed the item directly to the auction winner.

Jennifer set a one-week period for the auction and listed a starting price for each item equal to about one-third or one-half of the retail value. People entered their bid along with their name and e-mail address in the comment section of the item they wanted.

Jennifer chose not to specify how much higher each bid needed to be, but found most people were generous. At the close of the auction, seventy of the items had sold and raised $1,200 for the adoption fund. Jennifer e-mailed each of the winners with payment instructions and then organized the shipment of all the items.

Carolyn and Kiel Twietmeyer used an online auction to raise money for the adoption of their fourteenth (yes, you read that right) child—Isaac from Ukraine. More than 160 items were donated to the fifteen-day auction. The auction was mostly managed by friends of the Twietmeyers who got pictures from the item donors, created the postings, and helped contact all the winners.

Amount Raised: $6,000

The Elder family, who are adopting from Taiwan, listed sixty items in their online auction—all donated by people whom Angela Elder contacted via websites and blogs. The auction ran for a week. When there were twenty-four hours left, Angela added a new post with a list of items that hadn't been bid on to encourage her readers. Angela says keeping organized was the key! She used a spreadsheet to track the donor's name, item, minimum asking price, final bid, winner's e-mail address, shipping info, and payment information.

Amount Raised: $1,000

Christopher and Jennifer listed over seventy items in their online auction. Jennifer reached out to several of her favorite interior design bloggers to see if they would blog about the auction. While only two or three wrote blog posts, many of them agreed to advertise the auction via Facebook or Twitter. On one day, they had over 25,000 hits.

Amount Raised: $2,600

Online Giveaways

Blog giveaways are a fun way to raise money and can be as simple or complex as you want. However, before we dive into some examples, there are a few things you should know.

Legalities of Giveaways

Giveaways or raffles can present a problem. If they meet the legal IRS definition of "gaming," they are subject to state gambling laws. (For a list of these go to: rafflefaq.com/united-states-raffle-laws/) Some states allow nonprofit organizations to hold raffles, but that only helps you if you have a fund-raising grant tied to your raffle and donations are made to the organization. So first, check with your state laws.

Because of the varying state gambling laws, PayPal policy prohibits the use of their service in conjunction with any raffle. Obviously people are still using it and many get away with it. But several families I interviewed had PayPal accounts frozen and were forced to refund every transaction. Many donors then mailed the family a check, but obviously this is a huge headache.

Like PayPal, most online payment tools make raffle payments off-limits because it's too hard to regulate where it is or isn't legal and what state the donors live in. There are a couple of online raffle organizations, but they require you to get the necessary city and state permits, which may not be worth your time.

Your alternative is to have people mail you checks or, if you are doing a lot of in-person selling, you could sign up for a SquareUp card reader (squareup.com/) and run people's debit or credit cards via their smart phone app. You can also enter card numbers manually in the app if people gave them to you over the phone. (SquareUp charges a 2.75 percent transaction fee.)

If you want something less time-consuming, choose one or two popular items you think would be most appealing—electronics like a Kindle Fire HD, iPad, or iPod are popular.

With a little more time, you can gather a collection of items to give away and either choose to give the whole package to one winner or draw names for each item. Or you might have a series of giveaway contests for one item at a time. It's completely up to you.

Instead of paying for the prizes, see if you can get a business or individual to donate some items. Some families use airline or other "point programs" to acquire giveaway items so that all the money raised goes directly toward the adoption. If you have friends who are photographers, hair stylists, massage therapists, or offer other services, ask if they would donate a gift certificate to the cause. Check around and see if any friends have season tickets to the local professional sports team and would be willing to donate their seats to a game. The possibilities are endless. (If you get a ton of items, then you may want to try an online auction instead.)

Lara Dinsmore collected over thirty-five items that became one huge prize pack in her "Give Thanks Giveaway" held during the Thanksgiving holiday. By sponsoring a piece of "the pie" for $10, donors were entered in the drawing. People who purchased an adoption T-shirt received three additional entries. Donors received an additional entry if they shared the giveaway via social media.

Everything in the prize pack was donated by friends and other adoptive families.

Amount Raised: $470

Kryste decided to raffle off an American Girl Doll, allowing the winner to choose the specific doll. At first, she wasn't sure how successful the idea would be, hoping to clear $100 after purchasing the doll. A $10 donation to their adoption fund equaled one entry; a $25 donation equaled three entries. She asked friends and family to share the fund-raiser on Facebook. In one week, the blog received more than three thousand hits. Kryste received eighty donations and was totally blown away by the success of the giveaway.

Amount Raised: $2,375

Freezer Pleaser Fund-Raiser

This idea was shared by an attendee at one of my breakout sessions at the Christian Alliance for Orphans Summit. Originally done for a Junior Auxiliary community club, it translates well to an adoption fund-raiser.

A former club member who worked for Sears arranged to have a small chest freezer donated (value of about $125). If you know someone who works for a place like Sears, Best Buy, or Home Depot, see if he or she can connect you with a store manager. If a store can't donate, perhaps you could get an item at-cost?

Next, thirty women prepared a freezer meal. (There are hundreds of blogs devoted solely to freezer cooking, so recipes are easy to find.) Make sure each meal is labeled well and includes cooking directions.

The Junior Auxiliary raffled off the freezer with a month's worth of meals, selling raffle tickets for $5 each or five for $20. Most people chose to buy five tickets. Each member of the Junior Auxiliary (thirty of them) sold tickets face-to-face and collected funds. Living in a small town, they also set up a table in front of the high school football and softball games. The raffle drawing was held during the homecoming football game.

Amount Raised: $7,000

Deanne's family raised $2,800 for their adoption using this idea. An independent appliance store agreed to sell the freezer at-cost, but when the raffle was done and Deanne went to pay for the freezer, the owner donated it. Numerous people told Deanne they would enter another freezer meal raffle, even if only for the meals.

Rochelle and Tony Franco enlisted the help of friends to sell their freezer raffle tickets. Rochelle put several dozen tickets in fifteen brightly colored envelopes and printed directions on the front. She gave these to friends who then sold tickets at their churches, workplaces, and the local university. The Francos received a used freezer as a donation and friends filled it with ten meals. A few days before the prize drawing several local business donated gift cards and small prizes so there could be more than one winner. The Franco's estimate selling between seven hundred to eight hundred tickets at $5 each. They also received a $1,500 donation, which brought their freezer fund-raiser total to $5,170.

One tip: don't put the meals *in* the freezer. Let the winner pick up the freezer and then you can deliver the frozen meals separately.

Online Fund-Raising Tools

Several microgiving and online fund-raising organizations exist specifically to help adoptive families. Some just provide the added exposure, while some provide tax benefits to donors.

Pure Charity

Pure Charity began as a way to "unite individuals, nonprofits, and businesses in order to fund projects dealing with the causes and nonprofits you care about."

In partnership with hundreds of online retailers (Walmart, Old Navy, Target, Apple, Expedia, and so on), Pure Charity participants earn giving rewards for their online purchases and donate to any of several thousand projects listed on PureCharity.com.

People can also make direct donations to any cause listed.

In May 2013, Pure Charity launched a fund-raising platform to help adoptive families who have already raised several hundred thousand dollars (purecharity.com/how-it-works/individuals /adoption-fundraising/).

The process of setting up a Pure Charity fund-raiser is simple and only takes twenty to thirty minutes. Pure Charity created several videos to walk you through the process. You can upload pictures, videos—whatever helps you tell your story.

When you're done, embed their widget on your blog and use their social media sharing tools to spread the word.

The bulk of your donations will probably come from direct donations rather than shopping rewards. However, especially if you start early in your process, there is good potential in the shopping reward, since it has a snowball effect. When you sign up for Pure Charity you receive a referral link used to invite others to join, including an easy tie-in to Facebook. Anyone who joins your "Advocate Network" and makes purchases via Pure Charity adds money to your reward account as well. If their friends join, you earn more, and if their friends join, you earn even more.

Direction donations made by family and friends are tax deductible. Money from your Pure Charity fund-raiser is paid directly to your agency, so set your fund-raiser goal for your agency expenses only (not travel). You can set up a separate travel fund-raiser by partnering with Pure Charity and Fly for Good (purecharity.com/how-it-works/individuals/travel-fundraising/).

Pure Charity charges a 5 percent fee on fund-raisers to cover the cost of credit card fees and administration. You can add that amount to your overall fund-raising goal.

Of course when your adoption is complete, you'll still be earning Pure Charity rewards. You can give to one of the more than six hundred projects on the site or another family's adoption fund-raiser.

Ali and Josh saved for several years before beginning their adoption from Uganda and had enough to afford the process. But when friends and family kept asking how they could help, the couple came up with a creative way to use the Pure Charity fund-raising platform. Whatever donations were made, the couple donated an equal amount to three projects: the orphanage their child came from, other adoptive families needing financial assistance, and a water well in the area of Uganda their child was from. Their fund-raising goal of $20,000 was exceeded with 129 people donating over $25,000.

Give1Save1

Beth Cupitt started the Give1Save1 movement with a simple idea. Every week a new adoptive family is featured and people are asked to give $1. Obviously sometimes people give more. In the first four months, Give1Save1 raised $22,000 for sixteen adoptive families.

Give1Save1 is not a nonprofit so donations are not tax deductible. But, if you have a fund-raising grant established through another avenue, Give1Save1 directs donors to the correct payment spot.

Adopt Together

Adopt Together is crowd-funding at its simplest. Adoptive families create a profile and specify their fund-raising goal. A page is created where friends and family can donate. Adopt Together passes on 100 percent of the donations to families and does not take an administration fee (adopttogether.org).

Village to Village International

Village to Village International allows adoptive families to create an online profile and set a fund-raising goal. Although donations can be given in any amount, Village to Village focuses on getting donors to commit to $10 monthly donations. All donations go directly toward a family's adoptive costs (villagetovillageintl.com).

There are also several fund-raising sites that aren't adoption specific and don't provide tax benefits but can be used for fund-raising:

- youcaring.com (no administrative fee)
- gofundme.com (5 percent fee)
- fundrazr.com (Uses PayPal and Facebook to gather donations. Charges a 5 percent fee plus the PayPal fee)
- razoo.com (4.9 percent fee)

CHAPTER SIXTEEN
DEBT-FREE ADOPTION IS POSSIBLE

"Abraham named the place Yahweh-Yireh (which means 'the LORD will provide')." (Genesis 22:14). Abraham was given an impossible task. The son he had longed for, waited for, was to be sacrificed. Not knowing what lay ahead, Isaac asked his father on the journey up the mountain where the sheep was for their sacrifice. "God will provide a sheep for the burnt offering," Abraham answered.

Abraham knew God would provide, but did he know how? Would God have him kill Isaac and raise him from the dead so he could fulfill God's promise of many descendants? Without knowing the "how," Abraham still knew God would provide. He obeyed and followed through on God's instructions until, at the very last second, he was stopped by God's command and a sacrificial lamb was provided.

God is the Great Provider.

Sometimes He provides through huge, mind-blowing, miraculous circumstances.

Can you imagine a nineteen-year-old paying for the entire cost of your adoption? When God placed adoption on their hearts, Joe and Christie Darago learned that adopting from South Korea would cost three quarters of their annual salary. They knew they didn't want to go into debt and assumed it would take years for them to adopt. So the Daragos started a small savings account with $100, prayed, and asked friends and family to do the same.

Fifteen years ago there weren't many adoption grants available, and the Daragos felt completely overwhelmed by the cost. Knowing

God's call was clear, they prayed for a miracle. Never did they imagine a young college student would choose to pay for their adoption out of her trust fund. Christie said,

> She got together with my husband and her dad on December 23 and with many tears, shared that God was leading her to pay for our adoption. We were blown away and truly viewed this as a miracle. We started the adoption process officially in January of 1999 and our daughter, Sydney, came home in July of 1999. The process went incredibly fast and we are so thankful that a nineteen-year-old girl was open to God's leading and that He provided for us in such a miraculous way.

Seven months later their daughter Sydney, now seventeen, was home.

Recently, the Daragos learned about a girl in Thailand through an e-mail from their previous adoption agency. The eleven-year-old girl had thirty days to find a family. This time, with social media at their disposal, the couple was able to spread the word about their adoption more easily. They held a garage sale that netted $3,000 and received $2,000 from their church. Joe took on some side jobs to bring in extra cash.

Once again God showed up in miraculous ways and through the support of many generous friends they raised the entire $31,000 needed in just a few short months.

Of course for every jaw-dropping miracle story there are a dozen of couples who penny-pinch, work overtime, and fund-raise for years to raise the funds they need. Don't let the absence of a miracle check in your mailbox lead you to a place of disbelief or discouragement. It is often during this time of waiting for God to meet our needs that we get to know Him better.

David and Erica Shubin have five children, two of whom were adopted from Ethiopia. Their first adoption of then three-year-old Silas is a story of sacrifice and God's faithfulness. Shortly before God called them to adopt, the Shubins had put their house on the market and started to build a 3,900-square-foot "dream home." Erica says not only did God call them to adopt, but He called them to give up everything to follow His call. And not just sacrificing Starbucks. It meant the dream home. After much fasting and prayer the Shubins took their house off the market and pulled out of their dream home.

Two days after they made that decision, the Shubins received a life-changing call. At one time the Shubins thought they might owe $10,000 from a car accident that happened two years ago, involving Erica and the children. Instead she and the kids each received a settlement for medical bills, damages, and pain and suffering. Erica's portion of the settlement amounted to half of what was needed to fund their adoption.

The Shubins still needed $12,000 and anticipated they might need it quickly as they were part of a pilot program. Even the Shubin children sacrificed as they volunteered to give up their savings to help bring their brother home.

Then David was laid off from his job. Erica admits she was frustrated and couldn't imagine what good could come of this change.

"My sorrow was short-lived. I knew the One who owned it all and even through this trial I *knew* God had called us to adopt. He wouldn't abandon us now. Even in this He had a plan. He knew the end of the story. I was simply to trust. Walk. Obey. We did. We waited. We prayed. We waited some more," said Erica.

His former company denied David the quarterly bonus check he would have received just days after he was laid off. Erica filled out a grant application for Show Hope, feeling as if there were no other options. But not too many days later they received a call from the HR department. The bonus check had been deposited to their bank account. The amount was almost exactly what was needed to pay the family's referral fee. One month later David had a new job.

In January 2008 they received their final approval by the Ethiopian courts and all that remained was travel expenses. Erica's sister-in-law held a fund-raiser on her blog asking readers to donate $5. Those small donations covered meals in-country and Ethiopian visas. But the cost of plane tickets loomed in front of them.

Then the Shubins received a notice that they needed to do something with David's 401(k) account with his former employer. They had forgotten about that asset. The amount wasn't huge, but it covered their need. Continuing with their theme of giving up everything to follow the call, the Shubins cashed in the 401(k) account.

"We sought the Lord and asked for direction. Both of us felt the Lord asking us to trust Him with everything. So we did what many people in this world would call *crazy* and we cashed out that account. Our travel would be paid for. We didn't have any leftovers, we didn't have any excess, but we had enough. God is so good," Erica said.

Silas came home in February of 2008. Two years later the Shubins started the process to adopt four-year-old Zahra. But this time they would have to fund-raise along with sacrificing and saving. On her blog Erica wrote, "This is new ground and it's humbling. Yet we are confident that God will provide again and He has asked us to call on our friends and family to participate in a real adoption adventure."

For the next thirteen months the Shubins' persevered and worked diligently to raise the $26,000 they needed. A Facebook fund-raising drive raised $1,460 to kick off their fund-raising and pay for their home study. Friends held garage sales; Erica found and sold Africa-shaped cookie cutters and Uganda bead necklaces. The kids sold lemonade, cookies, and jewelry to help bring their sister home. They used a puzzle fund-raiser to encourage donations via their church. Eventually they were given a $3,000 matching grant they received from Lifesong for Orphans. And shirts…they sold *lots* of shirts. At least a couple hundred.

They mailed out baby bottles to friends for a "Change-4-a-Life" fund-raiser collecting spare change. Other adoptive families and ministries donated adoption gear—T-shirts, hats, bags, and jewelry—for a "Dress for a Cause" giveaway that outfitted an entire family with cool wearables. The giveaway raised over $900.

Erica blogged tirelessly about their fund-raising efforts. "I have to admit I get weary. It's a lot of work. If I lose focus on the one who owns it all, my King, my Savior, my Redeemer, I'm quickly panicked. *But* it's not my job to worry about where the money will come from. He already knows. He's got it figured out and He has it all under control. I choose to rest there," she wrote in a blog post.

Zahra came home in April 2011.

Danny and April adopted an eleven-year-old boy and a thirteen-year-old girl from Ukraine in 2012. They saved a bit of money on their $34,000 adoption by choosing to stay in-country between the required appearances rather than pay airfare for multiple trips. They also negotiated a good rate on a short-term apartment, fixed a lot of their own meals, and used public transportation rather than taxis. Still, with only $5,000 in savings to use, they had to work hard to raise the other $29,000 during their six-month process.

"We had messed up with money so much in our past and we are finally debt-free (except for our mortgage) that we were *not* about to take a step backwards," April said.

The family used Facebook and personal letters to ask for direct donations after hearing from friends who had been successful with this avenue. They raised over $14,000 this way. An online auction netted $1,750; $200 came from a car wash; and another $800 came from a rummage sale/bake sale.

Danny sold his high-end drum set for $3,600—well below its value but the amount provided the quick cash they needed. A grant for $10,000 was also a huge help.

The final piece of the puzzle was a God-provided increase in their income through unusual circumstances. As the owner of a small contracting company, Danny was approached by a friend who was a roofer and was looking for someone to take over his business so he could retire. He offered a profit-sharing arrangement that allowed the family to only pay him out of whatever increase in income they had. The situation was a win-win for both, and helped the family bring home their children without incurring any debt.

Kenny and Catherine Besk, otherwise known as the "karaoke couple" set out to adopt debt-free from Ethiopia. "We just knew that if God was calling us to adopt, that He was going to have to provide. We had never planned to adopt, and we both felt that we were directly asked to do so by God, so we felt confident that He would provide for us. Now, that didn't mean that we didn't have to work for it. We worked hard for a long time!" Catherine said.

They originally estimated their adoption would cost $32,000, but changes to the Ethiopia adoption process increased that. Ethiopia added a requirement for adoptive parents to be in-country for the court date, which added travel costs. New safeguards put in place and longer processing times by the Ethiopian government also slowed the process dramatically. This meant paperwork renewals, home study updates, and other costs that meant their adoption costs would be closer to $40,000.

Although their household income looks good on paper, the Besks live in an expensive area of the country and only had $300 in savings when they felt called to adopt. Catherine admits that they didn't know if adopting without debt would be entirely possible.

By far their most successful fund-raisers involved asking boldly for people to become part of their story and give. The Besks mailed out about two hundred letters but also used their blog and social media to spread the word. Catherine says they tried to make fund-raising fun by offering different incentives or prizes such as the "Tag the Bag Fund-Raiser" or puzzle pieces. Within the first seven months God provided $16,000.

Kenny sold his motorcycle for $2,500, yard sales and Craigslist added $2,700, a benefit concert raised $1,700, and of course the now famous karaoke party raised $1,300. They also received $1,250 from the Deputy Sheriff's Association (Kenny works in law enforcement). A Zumba party and two photo shoot auctions brought in a little over $1,000.

Over the three-plus years of their adoption, God provided every penny the Besks' needed to bring Matthew home.

Rodney and Stacy Kennedy admit that the cost of adoption caused them to hesitate a bit at first. "But when we prayed, it was abundantly clear that we were to step out in faith…and God provided *exact* amounts *every* step of the way!" Stacey said.

Their private infant adoption cost them approximately $15,000. They were already living debt-free and committed to staying that way through their adoption. Their biggest fund-raiser was a Both Hands Foundation project that brought in over $10,000. The Kennedys used that opportunity to send out letters with their entire team. News coverage of their event actually increased donations, and Stacy says that most of the money came in after their work day.

The Kennedys also held two different garage sales that raised $3,000. They also made use of Amazon's affiliate program and invited people to make Amazon purchases via their link. They included business cards with their Christmas letters, which they mailed early enough to take advantage of people's holiday shopping. Approximately $3,000 was added to their fund this way.

Curtis and Carrie Honeycutt started their adoption from Ghana in January of 2012. Curtis admits the $35,000 cost deterred him a bit but they plunged headlong anyways. They set out to adopt debt-free from the beginning.

"We had heard of people taking out loans, which, to me, would be a last-ditch effort. I just didn't think it was necessary," Curtis said.

The Honeycutts sent out more than two hundred hard copy letters to friends and family and received over $7,000 in donations. Adding social media and their blog to the mix, they ended up receiving over $22,000 total in a period of five months. Even though more donations came through electronic asks, the Honeycutts still felt a hard copy letter was important to make sure no one was missed.

The Honeycutts received a matching grant of $4,000 from Hands for Hope and Lifesong for Orphans and used Razoo to make online giving easy. Razoo then forwarded the money to Lifesong. After that goal was reached, the family then approached several friends about donating to a matching fund and ended up with $3,000, which doubled to $6,000. A garage sale, frozen yogurt fund-raiser, and Etsy shop sales brought close to $4,000.

To get the guys involved, Curtis challenged his friends to give the total amount of points scored during the big Oklahoma U. v. Texas game. A final score of 63-21 meant several gifts of $84 into their fund. Curtis said this engaged several guy friends who were sports fans but might not otherwise have donated toward their adoption.

During a "fund-raising funk" Curtis stumbled upon another fund-raiser. When he shaved his beard leaving only his mustache, two of his friends told him they'd do anything if he would keep the mustache for a week. Curtis challenged them to raise $1,000 in 24 hours, then they had a deal. #FreeTheStache was born and an "obnoxious social media blitz" brought in $1,300. "This engaged many of my goofball friends who like ironic hipster mustaches, but might not otherwise give toward our adoption," Curtis said. When the week was done Curtis created an in memoriam video remembering the life of his mustache as a thank-you to the donors.

The Honeycutts had set a goal of raising their entire fund by the end of 2013, only four months after they began the process. As Christmas passed they were just $738 short of their goal. With one specific ask on social media, someone gave the entire amount within five minutes.

Six families, six completely different stories. There is no "one way." The God who created our amazing universe cannot be put in a box. His creativity knows no limits and His provision is without question.

What will your story be?

CHAPTER SEVENTEEN
ADOPTION TAX CREDIT

The federal adoption tax credit, first introduced in 1997, benefits families who adopt through foster care, domestic or intercountry adoption. Over the years the rules and amount have changed and the credit was always temporary. As each expiration neared, pleas where made and an extension of the credit would be tacked on to some random legislation. Thankfully, the adoption tax credit is now a permanent part of the American Taxpayer Relief Act of 2012.

For adoptions finalized in 2014, the tax credit was $13,190 per child for "qualified adoption expenses." Each year that amount will increase slightly for inflation, usually a couple hundred dollars. If your family's modified adjusted gross income is above $197,880, the tax credit amount you are eligible for is decreased. If it is over $237,880, you will not be eligible for the credit. (The credit amount you are eligible for is determined by the year you finalize your adoption. If your income falls below $197,880 in subsequent years, it does not increase the amount you can receive.)

Remember the credit amount is *per child*. So if you adopt three children, you are eligible for up to $39,570—if you have that much in qualified expenses.

Qualified adoption expenses include:

- Adoption fees
- Attorney fees
- Court costs

- Travel expenses while away from home
- Re-adoption expenses (international adoption)

An example of non-qualifying expenses would be paying for housing for a birth mother in a domestic adoption. Buying a new minivan to fit your larger family doesn't count either.

There is one exception to the "qualified expenses" rule if you adopt a special-needs child (as defined by your state) from the foster care system. Those families qualify for the full amount of the tax credit regardless of actual expenses. This is helpful because families who adopt from foster care generally have little to no expense but can still claim the full $13,190 tax credit. Your child must be declared special needs on your Adoption Assistance Eligibility Determination Subsidy Agreement in order to qualify.

Receipts

During your adoption keep copies of all your receipts. Every time you get a paper notarized or have to pay a fee, get a receipt. Save them in one spot. If you have a scanner I recommend scanning copies into your computer. If your receipts are printed on the rolled receipt paper (like you get at a fast food restaurant) be sure to copy it because they will fade. After your adoption is complete, ask your agency or attorney for a complete itemized receipt. If you travel internationally for your adoption, it may be difficult to get receipts for every single meal, but collect what you can. If you don't get a receipt, make a note of the date, place, and amount spent.

When you file for the adoption tax credit depends on the type of adoption. For international adoption you cannot claim the adoption credit until the year your adoption is finalized. When your adoption is considered final varies by country. In Ethiopia, it is the day the Ethiopian courts approve your adoption, which can be weeks or months before your child comes home. In other countries it may be during your trip to pick up your child. Or it may be after you are back in the States. Your agency can answer this question for you.

Likely you will be incurring expenses for a year or more before you can file for the credit. This is also true for special-needs adoptions.

Private, domestic adoptions are a little different. You can claim the credit (for qualified expenses) before finalization, but you have to wait until a year after you incurred the expenses. If you had adoption expenses in 2014 but have not finalized the adoption by the end of 2015, you can still claim those expenses when you file 2015 taxes. If you then finalize the adoption in 2016, you would include any expenses incurred in 2015 and 2016 when you file your 2016 taxes.

How It Works

A tax credit is different from a tax deduction, which is what more people are familiar with. A tax credit goes dollar-for-dollar against your tax liability or what you owe the federal government in income taxes. Of course the actual calculations are a bit more complex but in order to explain it I'm simplifying these examples.

For example, Family A had $5,000 in income tax withheld from their paychecks during the year. Before filing for the adoption tax credit, their tax returns show them receiving a refund of $2,000. This means their actual tax liability was $3,000. The adoption tax credit zeroes out the $3,000 they owe so they receive a total refund of $5,000. They have now used $3,000 of their adoption tax credit and can carry the balance forward in the next year.

Family B had $5,000 in income tax withheld but when completing their taxes discovered they owed an additional $2,500 for a total tax liability of $7,500. After including their adoption tax credit (assuming they qualify for the complete amount) they would receive a refund of $5,000 and not owe the additional $2,500. Family B has now used $7,500 of their adoption tax credit.

Since the adoption tax credit only goes against your liability, most families won't qualify for the full credit the first year. The good news is that you can carry the credit forward for five years. If your adoption finalizes in 2015 you have until 2020 to use up your credit.

But what if you have no tax liability? Should you still file for the adoption tax credit? Absolutely! You never know what the next five years will bring. Perhaps two years after your adoption your income changes dramatically and you now have $5,000 in tax liability. If you didn't claim the adoption tax credit in the original year (and each year after), you have to go back and amend two years of taxes in order to get your $5,000 refund.

Grant Families

If you received money from a grant organization, this amount must be deducted from your total expenses before applying the tax credit. If you don't do this, your return will almost always get sent back by the IRS. Grant money generally goes to your adoption agency, so have them show it as "income" on your itemized bill. If you received a large amount of grant money (which would include any fund-raising grants or a Both Hands project), you may not qualify for the full credit.

Examples

Family 1
    Total adoption expenses—$25,000;
    Grant money received—$15,000;
    Remaining qualified expenses—$10,000.
    Family 1 can only claim $10,000 of the adoption tax credit

Family 2
    Total adoption expenses—$25,000;
    Grant money received—$7,000;
    Remaining qualified expenses—$18,000.
    Family 2 can claim the full $13,190 credit.

Filing the Return

As of the writing of this book, the IRS Form 8839 that is used for the adoption tax credit cannot be e-filed so you must mail your federal tax return. The first year you submit your documentation as well. It is important that you have every piece of documentation to avoid a delay with your refund. Using a red marker, write the primary household member's social security number on the top of every piece of documentation. You will need:

- Finalized adoption decree
- A home study/placement agreement
- All documentation of qualified expenses
- Adoption Subsidy Agreement (If claiming credit for a child declared special needs through state foster care.)

Mark and I always use personal tax software to file our taxes and it easily walks us through the steps of filing for the adoption tax credit. If you use a CPA or tax service to prepare your taxes, be aware that the majority of them are unfamiliar with the adoption tax credit. While they can certainly read tax code, I know more than one family whose normal CPA botched their return. Some families were told they don't qualify for the credit when, in fact, they do. Look for an adoption tax specialist.

If you are eligible for a refund *before* the adoption tax credit, you might want to file your return first without the adoption credit. This allows you to e-file and receive your standard refund quickly. Tax returns requesting the adoption tax credit take longer to review and process and many families have been asked for further documentation. Sometimes it has taken months to see the refund and there's no point holding up all your money. Once you receive your refund, immediately file an amended tax return claiming the adoption tax credit and submit it with the required documentation.[1]

Failed Adoptions

What if you incurred adoption expenses and then the birth mother changed her mind? In most cases, if the failed adoption is followed by a successful adoption, you can still claim the expenses of the failed adoption. However, it only counts as one adoption and so the maximum $13,190 applies. Talk with an adoption tax specialist.

State Adoption Benefits

Many states offer a tax benefit (deduction or credit) for adoption. In most cases it is a one-time benefit and a much lower amount.

Obviously, the adoption tax credit does not help you pay for your adoption expenses on the front end. It can help you replenish the savings account you drained. Or perhaps upgrade that junker car you bought when you sold your luxury sedan for your adoption fund. Or, if you think a second adoption might be in your future, put it in a savings account and let it grow. Or maybe you use some of it to help other adoptive families. If you took out an adoption loan, by all means, use your refund to pay it off ASAP!

Making the Adoption Credit Refundable

Remember how the adoption tax credit used to have to be renewed every few years? In 2010, with the credit set to expire, it was included as part of the Affordable Care Act and extended for two more years. The astounding thing was that the credit was made "refundable." This meant families received the entire amount of the adoption tax credit the year they filed, no matter what their tax liability. It was also determined that families who still had carryover credit would receive a refund in the remaining amount. I cried tears of joy over that one. We had $18,000 in tax credit remaining, and I thought we'd never see most of it since we have a low-tax liability.

As the deadline approached for the credit to expire again, several groups lobbied to make the credit permanent and refundable. We only won half the battle and the now-permanent tax credit is once again tied to your tax liability. The "Save the Adoption Tax Credit" group is still lobbying to make the adoption tax credit refundable and you can lend your voice to their efforts. Go to adoptiontaxcredit.org to find more information.

CHAPTER EIGHTEEN
GIVING BACK

It's done. You did it!

Your new child or children are home. Hopefully you've cocooned yourself for a while and allowed yourselves to ease into this new life. Jet lag, if you travelled internationally, is gone. New routines are established and the new normal is taking shape.

Congratulations!

Now what?

By all means take some time to relax and bond as a family. But my prayer is your adoption experience changed you forever.

You may never be able to look at a birth mom in crisis or a photo of an orphan in some foreign country the same way.

As adoptive parents, I believe we have a responsibility to do more than provide a family for the children we adopt. We are called to continue caring for the children left behind and moms and dads who don't have the resources to care for their kids.

One night during our adoption I remember suddenly feeling the weight and hopelessness of the orphan crisis. Literally millions of orphans don't have loving families. But what was I, one person, supposed to do? And did I really want to know the answer? Because, if I'm honest, part of me was afraid of the answer. Afraid it would mean doing something uncomfortable, even more "out there" then our adoption. Would God call us to move to Africa? What would He make me give up and what would I have to do? The fear can paralyze you.

Author and adoptive dad Tom Davis wrote in his book *Fields of the Fatherless*, "How do we overcome fear? We start by making others' pain a priority in our lives. People are eternal; fear is not. We change our lifestyles and start to give sacrificially of our time, energy, and resources to the fatherless. And then we do something daring to experience the joy and blessing of loving the poor."[1]

The good news is that there is *a lot* you can do. The orphan crisis (for simplicity's sake I'm including crisis pregnancies in this term) is a large puzzle. It was not caused by any one problem. The issue is not as simple as a child whose parents are dead or a birth mom who is sixteen and has no way to raise a child. The orphan crisis is a kaleidoscope of issues—poverty, education, healthcare, cultural expectations, and so on.

Likewise, the orphan issue cannot be solved by any one idea. Adoption won't solve it. Orphanages won't solve it. Pro-life pregnancy centers won't solve it. At least not alone. The solution has lots of pieces that, when working together, have the potential to make a real and tangible difference. The good news is that complex solution translates to hundreds of ways to get involved, and literally thousands of organizations that are doing something to prevent and care for orphans. Like fund-raising, there are so many options we can find something to do to help. There is no excuse.

Volunteering

Donate supplies. Call your local Child and Family Services office and ask about opportunities to help. You might conduct a back-to-school backpack drive to equip foster kids for school. Sometimes caseworkers have families in need of particular items to provide adequate care for their children and avoid removal. You could assist in finding donations like cribs, mattresses, diapers, formula, and so on.

Mentor a foster child. Most states have mentoring programs, similar to Big Brothers Big Sisters, that pair you with a foster child. Having a stable, consistent adult investing in a child's life makes a huge difference.

Become a Court Appointed Special Advocate (CASA). These trained volunteers are assigned to foster children until they are placed in permanent homes. They advocate for the child in legal proceedings and ensure the child's rights and needs are being taken care of while in foster care. For many children, a CASA is the only constant presence in their lives while in the foster care system. Becoming an advocate requires thirty hours of training and then CASA volunteers spend on average of ten hours a month on a case.

Provide respite care for a foster family. A licensed respite care worker provides short-term care for foster children while the foster parents take a much-needed break or if a foster child is not allowed to accompany the family out of state on a trip. Foster families cannot leave their children with just any babysitter so a network of respite care workers is a huge support. Respite care workers are generally paid by the state.

Volunteer at a group home. Foster care group homes function more like a dormitory than a family, and there are many ways you can help. You can tutor kids after school, do clothing, shoe, and school supply drives, teach a life skills class, or just make regular visits to play with the kids.

Become a peer counselor at a crisis pregnancy center. Most crisis pregnancy centers operate on a solid base of volunteers, including specially trained peer counselors who meet with women facing life-altering decisions. If that's not for you, ask if you can help with office work, coordinating their baby/maternity donation room or organize fund-raising events.

Support foster and adoptive families. Come alongside foster and adoptive parents in your church and community. Pray for them, check in on them, bring meals, mow their yard. Even small things are extremely helpful, especially immediately after a new child placement. Remember that sometimes it's hard to ask for help, so think of something you can do and just do it. Don't wait for them to ask.

Advocate for kids. Find ways to spread awareness in your community. Bring The Heart Gallery, a traveling photographic and audio exhibit created to find forever families for children in foster care, to your church. Share Waiting Children on your blog or Facebook wall.

Giving

After our journey and working in both church ministry and non-profit orphan care ministry, I am a fan of organizations that run lean and provide maximum benefit for your financial gifts. I also look for maximum impact and future growth. Direct your gifts to either orphan care or orphan prevention. Both are pieces of the puzzle.

Orphan care includes the day-to-day care of orphans who have no family to care for them. These children may live on the streets, in orphanages, in church-based family homes, or with foster parents. *Orphan prevention* includes a huge spectrum of things from job creation, prenatal care, education, healthcare, and human trafficking prevention.

There are hundreds, probably thousands of organizations doing great work. The Christian Alliance for Orphans website includes a list of organizations that serves as a great starting place. Also, your adoption agency is hopefully doing something to care for orphans in the countries they work in outside of just adoption. Otherwise, here are a few organizations I'm personally fond of for a variety of reasons.

World Orphans has projects in fourteen countries, most of which are done through the local indigenous church. My husband and I both worked for World Orphans for a time and I love their foundation and model. It is exciting to see the churches in these countries being called to care for their orphans and provide for them so that maybe, some day, international adoption is not needed. World Orphans believes in family-style homes with small groups of children living with house parents. They also do orphan prevention work and provide a variety of ways for you to get involved (worldorphans.org).

The Adventure Project (TAP) believes we can end extreme poverty in our lifetime by reinventing how people give. Every quarter TAP focuses on one humanitarian issue affecting global poverty.

They identify low-cost, high-impact solutions and partner with the best organizations tackling these problems by developing products and services that improve communities, save lives, and create jobs. TAP then adds "venture" by championing and fund-raising for these causes, mobilizing a movement of volunteers to tell the stories. For example, a $20 donation sponsors a coal-efficient stove for a family in Haiti. That stove saves the family $220 per year in coal cost, allowing them to have more money to feed their family and send their kids to school. It also lowers the risk of respiratory disease, the number one killer of children under five in Haiti (theadventureproject.org).

Heartline Ministries in Port-au-Prince, Haiti, has several programs including a maternity center where expectant mothers can find medical care, support, education, and safe, sanitary conditions. They are helping moms and babies thrive and making a huge difference in their community (heartlineministries.org).

Beauty for Ashes Uganda works with single moms and widows in thirty-one villages in Uganda. Beauty for Ashes helps them join cooperatives, pooling resources as a group so they can become self-sustaining, while receiving business training and loans to help. They also provide short-term help with school fees, animals (goats, roosters, cows, and so on) and emergency medical funds. Beauty for Ashes desires to partner each village (thirty women in each cooperative) with advocates from across the United States for deeper relationships and care. Founded by adoptive mom Brandi McElheny and her Ugandan counterpart Akwango Anne Grace, 100 percent of all donations go directly to the field (no administrative fees are taken). They desire to empower the beautiful women of Uganda to keep their babies and build their lives (facebook.com/beautyforashesuganda).

Kidmia is a nonprofit organization in Ethiopia whose priority is to see orphaned and vulnerable children be reunited or placed with a gospel-loving Ethiopian family and to reach their highest potential in their native country. Kimia partners with local churches to dispel cultural myths and encourage Ethiopian families to provide a home for orphaned children. They also do extensive community outreach projects including food, healthcare, and education (kidmia.org).

The goal of **Food for the Orphans** is to make sure every orphan receives at least one nutritious meal per day. Working in thirteen countries, they supply the funds to purchase food, as well as ship large containers of dehydrated meals to various well-screened orphan care projects. They also train the orphan caregivers on diet and nutrition (foodfororphans.org).

Founded in 2010 by Kristen Welch, **The Mercy House** exists to provide alternative options for pregnant girls living in the slums of Kenya. The Mercy House aids young women in education, nutrition, housing, prenatal care, Bible study, counseling, and job skills for sustainable living. The Mercy House is run by Maureen, a graduate of Compassion International's leadership program. The program currently houses twelve young ladies and their babies with plans underway to purchase a second home (mercyhousekenya.org).

Safe Families for Children is a network of local U.S. agencies and churches committed to preventing child abuse and helping at-risk families escape crisis situations. Since 2005, Safe Families for Children has offered sanctuary to thousands of children, minimizing the risk for abuse or neglect and giving parents the time and tools they need to help their families thrive. The ultimate goal is to strengthen and support parents so they can become Safe Families for their own children (safe-families.org).

Pay It Forward

You've been there. You understand how daunting the financial obstacles to adoption can be. But odds are you also now know every single little bit helps. Every gift of $5, $10, or $20 you received during your adoption added up to an incredible amount.

That is the gift that you can pay forward, perhaps with the most ease. When an adoption fund-raiser crosses your Facebook page or you read a blog post about an adoptive family that is raising funds, by all means, buy a T-shirt, buy a bag of coffee, or just give. That $10 might mean skipping a lunch out that week (you might have gotten used to that during your adoption) but it means immeasurably more to that family. Or you can financially support one of the grant organizations listed in the appendix.

Use your voice and social media presence to share other families' fund-raisers. I've been overjoyed to see how my friends have responded to the needs of others when I have posted them.

If someone you know is adopting, reach out and ask how you can help. Can you gather garage sale donations? Or help them with their pancake breakfast?

Most of all, having walked the road before them, you can be a source of encouragement and hope for other families by simply sharing your story, letting them know you're praying for them, and sharing any helpful resources you found along the way.

You are now part of an amazing community of adoptive parents. Never did I imagine that adding two kids to our family would literally add hundreds of friends to my life. My husband laughs when I say, "My friend Jody—" and has to interrupt me and ask "Is this a real-life friend or an online friend?" For women, sometimes there is no difference. But there are dozens of women who started out as online friends—bloggers who were a great source of encouragement and information for me during our process—who I have had the privilege to meet in real life. They have written books, started nonprofit organizations, and encouraged hundreds, even thousands of other adoptive parents. They will cry with you, pray with you, send you funny texts, and post silly videos to your Facebook wall when you need encouragement.

You belong to this group now. There are a multitude of ways to find us—Facebook, Twitter, adoption conferences, blogs, and websites. Don't be afraid to reach out, to ask questions, to be transparent, to seek help when you need it, and give encouragement when you can give it.

CHAPTER
NINETEEN
OUR JOURNEY TO ETHIOPIA

I kept waiting for that miracle check to come in the mail that would pay a large chunk of our adoption. Well, not *really* but it sounds nice.

God definitely blessed us. First, Mark got a severance package from the church. We were not expecting this by any stretch of the imagination since it was his choice to leave. That check was the first confirmation that God was going to honor our commitment.

Then, we just got to *work*.

We applied for a couple of direct grants despite my assumption that we looked too good on paper. I did my best to explain our circumstances in a letter that accompanied each grant application but we were still denied. Of course knowing what I know now, I wish I had applied for a lot more grants.

I admit I became discouraged when we were turned down, and I wondered how God planned on working this whole debt-free adoption thing out.

We did get a fund-raising grant but to be honest, we weren't sure how best to use it. We were in a unique situation and Mark's unemployment made it a little difficult. We initially thought that he would have a new job within a few months. He took a three-week trip to Africa with one ministry but realized it wasn't what the Lord had for him at that moment. He could have applied for a job delivering pizzas or working part time but we, especially I, felt like he needed a break and a period of recovery.

So we didn't feel comfortable just asking for straight donations. We mentioned our adoption in our Christmas letter and gave a vague reference to adoption expenses and if our friends and family wanted to know how they could help us to let us know. In the end a couple of family members did donate and I'm grateful we had the tax write-off opportunity for them.

We had a few weekend "eBaypaloozas" where Mark and I photographed and listed items on eBay. Some were left over from the garage sale, some were from Mark's parents' house. We added at least another $1,000 to the adoption fund.

Mark put his bargain shopping to good use and bought and resold electronics, golf clubs, and so on. It became a part-time job for him.

My freelance design work brought in, by my best estimates, $8,000 for our adoption fund.

I wish I had kept better track of where all the money came from. All I know is that when we needed to write a check, the money was in our account. Every single time. Thankfully adoption expenses are spread out over a period of time.

Some of our best friends, Dustin and Jen, had started the Ethiopian adoption process seven months before us. They had a different agency and were on the waiting list for an infant. One day, early in our process, Jen had remarked, "Wouldn't that be cool if we could travel together? I'm going to start praying for that."

Thanksgiving Day I was a bundle of nerves, but giddy at the same time. In the recent weeks it seemed as if a large number of families were not making it through court on their first date. It's not completely unusual for it to happen, but the number of families having to wait seemed to have skyrocketed. Usually because of a missing piece of paper or a family member who didn't show up in court.

One moment I was completely confident we were going to pass court; the next I tried to temper my enthusiasm lest I be disappointed. God had been showing up in such a major way financially that it was kind of hard not to expect Him to get us through.

That night I took my cell phone upstairs and laid it on my night-stand with the ringer on as loud as it would go. I knew our agency caseworker would call or text the moment she knew something. With the time difference between the States and Ethiopia, that could be the wee hours of the morning.

Mark woke up at the crazy hour of 4:00 a.m. to hit the Black Friday sales. As usual, I didn't hear a thing when he left. When I first stirred at 6:30, I glanced at my phone. There it was—a text message from our caseworker sent at 4:31 a.m.: "It was early today!!! You have been approved!"

I let out a squeal before I quickly dialed Mark and told him the good news. I lay in bed for awhile, thinking I could go back to sleep. Ha! I finally got up and went downstairs, straight to the computer. All week I had worked on the announcement video for my blog—the first time I would be able to publicly share the kids' pictures and names. It had a clip of them singing from the very first video we saw as well as pictures and clips from a video update we got midway through the process. I typed up a quick message to go with it and hit the publish button. It was the most amazing feeling!

Passing court was an answer to prayer, but now the final agency fee was due and $8,000 in travel expenses were looming. With the income I made from freelance jobs and donations to our adoption fund, we were so close to our goal. We still needed $3,000.

Several months prior, I volunteered to redesign the website for our adoption agency. I had worked on it for several weeks when our case manager mentioned that the director said he would give us a discount on our agency fee for my work.

They never asked me how much I would normally charge for the job. I thought about giving them a figure, but I felt God telling me not to worry about it. Whatever they offered would be a bonus, even if it was only a couple hundred dollars. Nothing more was said.

A few days after we passed court, our case manager called and said the director was applying a $3,000 credit to our agency fee for the website redesign.

And there it was. Our complete adoption costs, miraculously provided for by God! Dustin and Jen passed court four days later. We would be traveling together!

Picking Up the Kids

It's hard to describe how it feels to go a year missing part of your family. At restaurants, I would think about how we'd need a bigger table. During worship at church, I would imagine Wendemagegn and Beza standing next to me in the dimly lit auditorium. At bedtime, I would imagine tucking in two more children. Those longings would be reality soon.

We arrived in Ethiopia on December 16 and spent several days visiting the ministry of Hope for the Hopeless with our friends. We were incredibly touched by the kids, and they still hold a special place in our hearts. We learned so much about joy and contentment from orphans that many view as needy. God used them to speak to us in a mighty way. On December 21 we separated from Dustin and Jen and went to our respective agency hotels.

We settled into the Bole Rock Hotel where we had a two-room suite with a small kitchenette. Hotel staff moved two twin beds into the living area for the kids and left us to settle in.

That night I slept surprisingly well despite the music coming from the fitness center next door and the prayers over the loudspeaker in the early morning.

We dressed and tried to eat breakfast although my stomach seemed to just lurch around in my torso.

Our driver picked us up about 10:30 and we drove the twenty minutes to the transition home in pretty much complete silence. I was too nervous to say much. It was a strange mix of anticipation and fear. Would Wendemagegn and Beza run and give us a hug? Would they be scared? Would they recognize us from the pictures we sent? Would they cry? Would we cry?

As the gates opened and the driver pulled his car into the courtyard, my eyes quickly scanned the faces in the crowd of kids sitting in the courtyard, but I couldn't find them. Surprisingly we weren't mobbed by the younger kids who seemed to be doing some school reciting with their day-to-day caregivers.

We sat in a room just off the courtyard with a couple small couches and chairs. It was obviously the designated "meet the family" room. After an excruciatingly long thirty minutes we were told that the kids were with the agency personnel at their final medical appointment required by the U.S. Embassy. Another hour crawled by.

A few moments later, Wendemagegn and Beza walked into the room where we waited. Shyly and quietly, they hugged us and sat as we made small talk, which isn't easy when you have the driver and the agency worker sitting there staring at you. I don't even remember what I said. I'm sure it was all completely inane and inadequate. Moments before they arrived I realized we had not brought one *single* thing with which to entertain them or break the ice—no ball, no candy, nothing. *Ugh!*

It was lunch time and so both kids went off to get their lunch. Beza brought it back to sit with us. Wendemagegn didn't return and we were told he went to finish a school exam. (He's still that dedicated to his schoolwork.)

We had a few pieces of paperwork to sign and then we finally left and headed back to our hotel to begin our new life together.

On the way back to the hotel we stopped and Mark bought a soccer ball—Wendemagegn chose yellow—while I waited in the car with the kids. The rest of the afternoon we put together small puzzles, played with toys, and colored. We ordered up pizza and French fries from the hotel restaurant. They had the best French fries we've ever had. Who knew you'd have to go to Ethiopia to get awesome fries?

We were pleasantly surprised at how much English the kids spoke and understood. (We would find out later that they didn't understand quite as much as they let on.) We were able to convey most of what we needed to with a few added hand motions for clarification.

The next morning the kids woke me up by singing "their" song—the "Good Morning" song they sang on that first video we saw of them that made me fall in love with them. I had never even thought about how one day they would sing it to me in person. I did my best to hold in my happy tears and not alarm them. They made their bed and placed their neatly folded pajamas on the pillow. (This ended *very* shortly after we got back to the States.)

After breakfast they wanted to watch a movie and picked out *Curious George*—they seemed to recognize it. Beza really got the physical humor in those kinds of movie and they laughed a lot. After that we went outside and played soccer, Frisbee, and blew bubbles. Beza loved to chase the bubbles and watch them float up into the air. Playing outside is when the kids were most comfortable and loosened up. We also made good entertainment for all the construction workers busy on the building behind us. At one point when Wendemagegn was near the far wall, one of them said something to him. He pointed to me and said "Mother." The man laughed and said to me, "Mother?"

"Yes. Mother, father," I said pointing to Mark. They just chuckled.

Friday evening we were back at the airport, meeting up with Dustin and Jen for the long journey home via Washington, D.C., and Denver. The kids were fascinated by the plane although Beza kept pointing to her stomach and looking uncomfortable. I'm not sure if she was actually motion sick or just not used to the way your stomach feels when the plane climbs. Regardless, we kept them entertained and *tried* to get them to sleep. We also made about a dozen trips to the bathroom.

Everything was going smoothly until we reached Washington, D.C. We disembarked and loaded on to the people mover that takes you to the baggage claim area. It was then that Beza burst into tears. I just hugged her to me and pretended to ignore the stares of three dozen people. When we got off we were able to sit down and talk with her. We tried, through Wendemagegn, to figure out if she was scared or sad or what but we didn't get much response. I'm sure it was all of the above coupled with extreme exhaustion.

A Wendy's hamburger, some French fries, and a movie on the portable DVD player seemed to settle her down. The kids didn't sleep again until our Denver- to-Phoenix leg—falling asleep before we even took off. Beza was so out that I thought I was going to have to carry her off the plane.

Touching down in Phoenix we were greeted by just a small crowd. Mark's mom and great-grandmother (his dad was out of town), my dad (my mom was in the hospital), and Stacey. Noah and Natalie, too, of course! They were so excited! I'm glad we kept our greeting crew pretty small. It's tempting after watching all those emotional homecoming videos to want a grand party yourself, but I'm glad I listened to my gut and kept it simple.

Beza's tears started again in baggage claim. Wendemagegn was goofing off with Noah and Natalie within minutes while we sorted out the luggage issues.

The First Few Months

We fed the kids some dinner and got everyone in bed by about 9:00 p.m. Mark woke me up about 4:30 a.m. with a teary Beza (he had been up and heard her). I climbed in her bed and just hugged her while she cried. After a while I realized that she was not falling back asleep. Thinking a distraction might help, we went downstairs and laid on the couch watching *Tom and Jerry*. Since Mark's jet lag had him wide awake, he relieved me and I went back up to bed until about 8:00 when he woke me up. Wendemagegn was crying this time, so Mark went to comfort him while I was on duty downstairs. This scene played out the same way for the next several days.

The next day the kids played happily, going from one thing to the next. They had the Nerf guns out, puzzles, K'nex, and Hot Wheels. They got along great, and the language barrier didn't really seem to be an issue. I don't think Noah and Natalie realized how much or little Wendemagegn and Beza understood; they just kept going and it seemed to work. I was not prepared for the pure exhaustion that would haunt us for the next week.

By dinnertime we were practically falling asleep in our plates. After about a week the kids were sleeping through the night, and Mark and

I felt a little more human. It was fortunate that Noah and Natalie were still on Christmas break. It gave us some time to start bonding.

We had already warned Noah and Natalie that the television, computers, and video games would remain off during the day for the first few weeks. We wanted them playing with their new siblings.

I had been warned that it might be difficult for Beza and Wendemagegn to figure out how to play the way Noah and Natalie did. After all, their entertainment was having the run of their neighborhood and playing extended games of hide and seek or hours of soccer. Sitting down and playing with Legos, Noah's favorite pastime, was completely foreign to them. So we played a lot of cards and spent lots of time at the park. Thank goodness Phoenix has beautiful weather in December.

For the first three weeks we were home, friends brought us dinner nearly every night. It was a wonderful blessing in the midst of our exhaustion, but it also revealed our first major problem—food. So many of the meals prepared so lovingly by friends went uneaten by Beza and Wendemagegn. We'd encourage them to take a bite and then let them fill up on plain pasta, fruit, and peanut butter sandwiches.

When the food delivery stopped and it was finally time for me to figure out what to prepare for dinner, I wanted to cry.

The challenge was finding foods they would eat. Pasta went over OK with a little oil and berbere (an Ethiopian spice that we bought in a large quantity). They also liked several kinds of fruit—bananas, apples, oranges, mangos. They ate fruit so fast I could barely keep us stocked. The third day we were home Mark calculated they were eating about $8 in fruit a day! So I began cooking the same meals I'd been cooking our family of four.

Beza would come into the kitchen to see what was cooking on the stove. She would put her face down just an inch from the pot and take several deep sniffs. Then she would raise her head, wag her finger at me and say "I no like that!" Of course she hadn't tried it, had no idea what it was, and no idea if she would like it, but once she got it in her head, it was impossible to get out. Pretty soon I learned to make sure she was occupied elsewhere during dinner prep.

Each night I would prepare the main dish and make sure there were several side items they liked. (We all ate a lot of fruit and pasta.) We asked them to take one bite of the new dish. If they didn't like it, they could fill up on the other items. They could also make themselves a peanut butter sandwich. I refused to be a short-order cook because I needed to keep my sanity.

They were rewarded for trying the new foods with dessert—one of those frozen tube popsicles you can buy in the large box and end up costing about 5 cents each. I would hit on something they liked about one out of every four tries. Slowly, but surely, we were able to add to the list of acceptable foods.

They would also look through the Amharic/English phrasebook and find foods they liked. This is how we discovered that they liked sweet potatoes and white (had to be white) corn.

At the end of three or four months I felt like we finally had reached a point where I had a variety of main dishes they liked and didn't need to approach each dinner prep with trepidation. They were also getting used to our style of food and seemed to be easier to please.

I sometimes laugh because all of a sudden they will declare their love for a food they've turned their nose up at for the last year. For months Wendemagegn would pick the green bell peppers out of dishes. Then one night I served chicken tetrazzini and he exclaimed, "Mom, what are these green crunchy things? You should put more of them in!" Now he wants green bell peppers on everything.

After more than six years home, they each have just a few foods they don't like. Wendemagegn won't eat hot dogs, sausage, or bacon. Beza doesn't really care for cheese except for on pizza. For a long time she'd complain if it was sprinkled on top of enchiladas while, at the same time, asking for seconds on several dishes she didn't realize had cheese mixed in. So if cheese is optional then it gets left off, but I don't change my recipes just to suit her.

As can be expected, the kids' grief came in waves. It was felt most often at night, a result of lying quietly and having time to think, I'm sure. Wendemagegn seemed to acclimate faster and after a few weeks there were no more tears from him. It took Beza several months before the grief subsided. It wasn't constant by any means; it would just pop up from time to time. She talked about going back to Ethiopia a lot and how much she missed her grandmother. There was one particularly unfun day when she was mad about something and declared she wanted to go back to "her other life."

Noah and Natalie returned to school a week after the kids got home. We had decided to keep Wendemagegn and Beza home for awhile, partly for attachment reasons, partly to see where they were education wise. I did some very basic school with them in the mornings using worksheets I printed from the Internet and those large curriculum workbooks you can buy for each grade level. Every day they would ask, "We go to school now, mom?" So ten days after Noah and Natalie went back to school, their siblings joined them. They settled in immediately and made fast friends.

They both receive nearly all A's with an occasional B. We were told their father was extremely smart, an engineer and one of the brightest in school. Obviously they take after him.

Siblings

Now, six years since we became a family, people always want to know how the kids get along.

Like normal siblings, they play great together one moment and drive each other nuts the next.

It's been interesting to see Beza and Wendemagegn's personalities come out and see how they fit into the family dynamic.

Noah is very much an introvert and an indoor guy. He would prefer to be reading, playing a video game, or building Legos. While he enjoys playing with other kids if they want to participate in one of those activities, he is perfectly content to play on his own. If he does engage with other kids in some sort of game on the trampoline, he is often the one orchestrating it and inventing all the rules.

Natalie is the social butterfly. While she enjoys reading and can play on her own, she would always prefer to be doing something with someone. She's not extremely athletic, but she enjoys being outdoors, jumping on the trampoline, or playing in the playhouse. She's quite talkative but always cheerful and very generous.

Wendemagegn is most like Natalie with the added athleticism. They can both be really silly and are usually going 100 mph. He is sensitive, caring, hardworking, and very generous. He makes friends easily, being the most easygoing of the bunch. But, like Noah, he is also kind of competitive.

Beza's personality is a combination of all three kids. She is also very athletic and active and loves to be involved in whatever Natalie and Wendemagegn are doing. But she also enjoys time alone to draw, write, or read. She and Noah have the most difficulty getting along, but that's because they are very similar. Both are pretty strong-willed, independent, and stubborn. Kind of like their mom.

We have our moments, but I don't imagine it's that different from the moments we would've had if we hadn't adopted; there are just more of them.

The best thing we did was have the kids share rooms. Bedtime is when Noah and Luke do most of their talking and goofing off. Sometimes a little too loudly. Lately I've come to realize that Beza also confides quite a bit in Natalie and I'm sure many of these conversations happen at night after the lights are off.

Parenting four is definitely harder than parenting two. There's twice as much chaos, twice as many kids to get to doctor's appointments and school activities. There's way more groceries to buy and way more messes to clean up. The good news is that there are more kids to help carry in the groceries, help cook meals, and clean up messes. There is also way more fun!

The time has passed more quickly than I ever imagined. I am still in awe of the fact that I get to raise these kids into adulthood and watch them flourish. I know God has big plans for their lives and for the rest of us as well.

APPENDIX

Grants

This list is certainly not exhaustive, but contains the most well-known grants. For a complete list, I recommend you visit Resources4Adoption.com and check into the Adoption Toolkit. Resources4Adoption is diligent about checking out new grant sources and following up with existing ones to make sure they are awarding money and are truly legitimate. The toolkit catalogs more than sixty grants and loans and makes it easy to sort them based on different requirements. At a glance you'll be able to decide which grants you should apply for.

A Child Waits Foundation

Specifically designed to help older children and children with special needs, the A Child Waits (ACW) Grant Program helps families pursuing international adoption of these special children. The adoptive child must be over the age of five or have a medical or developmental need that makes the child harder to place. A home study and referral are required before filling out the pre-qualification form available on their website. Grant money is paid directly to the service providers (adoption agency, travel agent, and so on) and is disbursed just before the family is due to travel. The application process takes two to four months. Grant amounts vary but do not exceed $5,000.

achildwaits.org

Application fee: None

Both Hands Foundation

By partnering with Lifesong for Orphans, the Both Hands Foundation offers a unique grant opportunity. Approved adoptive families solicit fund-raising sponsorship of a work day to benefit a widow in their community. Chapter 14 contains more details.

bothhands.org

Application fee: None

Funding Hope

Funding Hope provides financial matching grants in partnership with the local church to help Christian families adopt. Once a matching grant is awarded, the adoptive family must secure matching funds from its local church. This can be done through straight donations or the church or family's small group can choose to hold a fund-raiser.

funding-hope.org

Application fee: None

Gift of Adoption

Gift of Adoption awards grants to families in the process of domestic and international adoptions. You must have an approved and current home study from a licensed and accredited social worker. Those adopting internationally *must* use the services of a Hague-accredited adoption agency. Grants range from $1,000 to $7,500 with the average award being $3,500.

giftofadoption.org

Application fee: $50

God's Grace Adoption Ministry

Established in 1998, God's Grace Adoption Ministry (GGAM) uses matching grants to help adoptive families. Grants are available for Christian, two-parent families at any stage of the adoption process with a household income of $60,000 or less. Grant money is paid once a child (or children) is in the custody of the family and they

submit outstanding adoption expenses that GGAM pays. The average grant amount is $2,500.
ggam.org
Application fee: $10

Golden Dawn Adoption Assistance

Golden Dawn awards grants up to $2,000 to "Christian and Latter Day Saints couples" adopting children with special needs. They have awarded eighteen grants totaling $35,000.
goldendawnaa.org
Application fee: $20

Hand in Hand

Hand in Hand helps families with matching grants. A completed home study and application is required. All grant money is disbursed directly to service providers.
handinhandadopt.org
Application fee: None

Help Us Adopt

Private, domestic, international, and foster care adoptions are all eligible for grants from Help Us Adopt. Awarded twice a year in June and December, grants range from $500 to $15,000, depending on individual family situations. (Deadlines are in April and October.) You must have a completed home study. Priority is given to couples and individuals without children already in the home. Grant money is paid directly to service providers and must be used within one year.
helpusadopt.org
Application fee: None

His Kids Too!

His Kids Too! allows people to make tax-deductible donations toward your adoption expenses. They are open *only* to U.S. citizens adopting children from outside the United States. Funds can only be

disbursed to licensed adoption agencies, so independent adoptions do not qualify. No matching grants are available.
hiskidstoo.org
Application fee: None

Katelyn's Fund

Katelyn's Fund provides grants to Christian couples completing domestic or international adoptions. Applicants must have a completed home study and be interviewed by the board either in person or via conference call. Grants are typically $3,000 and given as funds allow.
katelynsfund.org
Application fee: None

Lifesong for Orphans

Lifesong enables friends and family to contribute to your adoption and receive a tax deduction by offering matching grants ranging from $1,000 to $4,000. Its goal is for children to be adopted into two-parent Christian families. Financial assistance is awarded based on need of the child, financial need of the parents, referral from and level of support from church leadership, leading of the Holy Spirit, and availability of funds. If accepted, families receive a fund-raising kit to help them raise funds during a specific date range. (Lifesong also helps churches administer adoption funds for their members.)
lifesongfororphans.org
Application fee: None

Lydia Fund

Available to Christian couples in the process of adopting internationally, applications for Lydia Fund grants must be made at least three months prior to travel. You may apply as soon as your home study and immigration paperwork process are underway. An interview is done before final approval. Selection for interviews is made within ninety days of application.

lydiafund.org
Application fee: None

One Less Ministries

One Less Ministries provides adopting grants to Christians (married or single) who are using a 501(c)(3) adoption agency.
onelessministries.org/adoptiongrant/
Application fee: None

Parenthood for Me

Grants are available to U.S. citizens pursuing adoption—either private or agency, either domestic or international. A completed home study is required. Families who already have children may apply but family size is taken into consideration during award decisions. Grant money is dispensed to the service provider.
parenthoodforme.org
Application fee: None

Room for One More Child

With no religious or marital requirements, Room for One More Child awards grants based on resources and priority is given to those demonstrating the greatest need. The application is available online and may be completed once you have your home study.
roomforonemorechild.org
Application fee: None

Saving Children, Building Families

Open to married couples with no religious requirements, Saving Children awards grants for international adoptions only.
savingchildren.net/
Application fee: None

Show Hope

Providing grants to Christian families and single parents, Show Hope has six application deadlines throughout the year. Applicants must have a completed home study and be in the process of adoption using a 501(c)(3) agency. Grants are awarded for both domestic and international adoptions. Application processing takes a minimum of ninety days, and priority is given to applicants with the greatest financial need.

showhope.org

Application fee: None

Sparrow Fund

The Sparrow Fund is a specialized grant designed to help internationally adopting families who would like to consult with medical professionals regarding their child's referral. These consultations are not covered by insurance so The Sparrow Fund was set up to assist families in paying for these services. Applications are accepted January through October.

sparrow-fund.org

Application fee: None

Some adoption agencies also have their own specific grants, so ask your caseworker. Here is a list of a few grant organizations that seek to help families in specific areas of the country or those in a specific targeted group. (*Note:* This grant list is informational and should not be construed as direct recommendations.)

Adoption Funds for Ministers—Southern Baptist Ministers and Missionaries (namb.net/SBC_Adoption_Fund_for_Ministers/)

Ibsen Network—Washington State (ibsenadoptionnetwork.com)

Kinsman Redeemer—Missouri (thekinsmanredeemer.org)

Kyle Reagan Foundation—Indiana (kylereagan.org)

Micah Fund—Minority children in Minnesota, North Dakota, South Dakota, Iowa, and Wisconsin (micahfund.org)

Topeka Community Foundation—Kansas (topekacommunityfoundation.org)

Books

Dave Ramsey, *Total Money Makeover* (Nashville: Thomas Nelson, 2009).

Mary Ostyn, *Family Feasts for $75 Per Week* (Birmingham: Oxmoor, 2009).

Rachel Masters, *Supper's on the Table, Come Home* (schallertel. net/~rmasters).

Karyn B. Purvis, David R. Cross, and Wendy Lyons Sunshine, *The Connected Child* (New York: McGraw-Hill, 2007).

Laura Christianson, *The Adoption Decision: 15 Things You Want to Know Before Adopting* (Eugene, OR: Harvest House, 2007).

Deborah D. Gray, *Attaching in Adoption: Practical Tools for Today's Parents* (London: Jessica Kingsley Publishers, 2012).

Deborah D. Gray, *Nurturing Adoptions: Creating Resilience After Neglect and Trauma* (London: Jessica Kingsley Publishers, 2012).

Gregory C. Keck and Regina Kupecky, *Parenting the Hurt Child: Helping Adoptive Families Heal and Grow* (Colorado Springs: NavPress, 2009).

Gregory C. Keck and Regina Kupecky, *Adopting the Hurt Child: Hope for Families with Special-Needs Kids: A Guide for Parents and Professionals* (Colorado Springs: NavPress, 2009).

Mary Ostyn, *Forever Mom: What to Expect When You're Adopting* (Nashville: Thomas Nelson, 2014).

Daniel J. Siegel and Tina Payne Bryson, *The Whole-Brain Child: 12 Revolutionary Strategies to Nurture Your Child's Developing Mind* (New York: Bantam, 2012).

Jean MacLeod and Sheena Macrae, *Adoption Parenting: Creating a Toolbox, Building Connections* (Warren, NJ: EMK Press, 2007).

Sherrie Eldridge, *Twenty Things Adopted Kids Wish Their Adoptive Parents Knew* (New York: Dell, 1999).

Susan TeBos, Carissa Woodwyk, and Sherrie Eldridge, *Before You Were Mine: Discovering Your Adopted Child's Lifestory* (Grand Rapids: Zondervan, 2011).

Russell D. Moore, *Adopted for Life: The Priority of Adoption for Christian Families and Churches* (Wheaton, IL: Crossway Books, 2009).

Arleta James, *Brothers and Sisters in Adoption: Helping Children Navigate Relationships When New Kids Join the Family* (Indianapolis: Perspectives, 2009).

B. Bryan Post, *From Fear to Love: Parenting Difficult Adopted Children* (Palmyra, VA: Post Institute, 2010).

Nancy Newton Verrier, *The Primal Wound: Understanding the Adopted Child* (Louisville: Gateway, 2003).

Mary Hopkins-Best, *Toddler Adoption: The Weaver's Craft* (London: Jessica Kingsley Publishers, 2012).

Judy M. Miller, *What to Expect from Your Adopted Tween*, 3d ed. (NliveN, 2014).

Kathleen Silber and Phylis Speedlin, *Dear Birthmother: Thank You for Our Baby*, 3d ed. (New York: Corona, 1998).

Amy Coughlin and Caryn Abramowitz, *Cross-Cultural Adoption: How to Answer Questions from Family, Friends & Community* (Washington, DC: Lifeline, 2004).

Barbara Katz Rothman, *Weaving a Family: Untangling Race and Adoption* (Boston: Beacon, 2006).

Marguerite Wright, *I'm Chocolate, You're Vanilla: Raising Healthy Black and Biracial Children in a Race-Conscious World* (San Francisco: Jossey-Bass, 2000).

Elisabeth O'Toole, *In On It: What Adoptive Parents Would Like You to Know About Adoption: A Guide for Relatives and Friends* (St. Paul: Fig Press, 2011).

Articles

"Top Ten Tips for Using the Internet to Find Prospective Birth mothers" by Creating a Family, creatingafamily.org/adoption-resources/top-ten-tips-for-using-the-internet-to-find-prospective-birth-mothers.

Conferences

Empowered to Connect website and conference, including great videos, a study guide to accompany *The Connected Child*, DVDs—empoweredtoconnect.org

Christian Alliance for Orphans Conference—christianalliance fororphans.org

Together for Adoption Conference—togetherforadoption.org

Websites

Adoption

adoptionattorneys.org
adoptivefamilies.com
adoptuskids.org
childwelfare.gov
davethomasfoundation.org
embryoadoption.org
resources4adoption.com
theadoptionguide.com
travel.state.gov/content/adoptionsabroad/en.html

Fund-Raiser Related Sites

147millionorphans.com
adoptionbug.com
adoptiontees.com
adopttogether.org
bothhands.org
cash4shooz.com
chromebuffalo.com
compelleddesigns.com
fundrazr.com
give1save1world.blogspot.com
gofundme.com
gracehavenhome.com
justlovecoffee.com

life2orphans.org
projecthopeful.org
purecharity.com
razoo.com
showhope.org
villagetovillageintl.com
youcaring.com

Adoption Tax Credit
adoptiontaxcredit.org
centralia-il-taxservice.com

Orphan Care
facebook.com/beautyforashesuganda
foodfororphans.org
heartlineministries.org
kidmia.org
mercyhousekenya.org
safe-families.org
theadventureproject.org
worldorphans.org

Meal Planning and Coupons
emeals.com
couponmom.com
coupons.com
couponsense.com
grocerygame.com

Adoption Travel
Adoptiontravel.com
adoptionairfare.com/
mkigrouptravel.com/

Adopt Without Debt Workshop

The "Adopt Without Debt" Workshop is a 2.5 hour presentation that includes: how to find more money in your budget, adoption grants, and creative fund-raising ideas. A shorter one-hour presentation title "Creative Fund-Raising Ideas" is also available. I'm available to adoption agencies, church ministries, and nonprofit organizations. For more information on fees and availability, please e-mail julie@juliegumm.com.

What Others Are Saying

"Julie Gumm has been helping our families for years by providing innovative and practical ways to fund their adoptions. She encourages men and women to think about how they can save more, bring in extra income, and pool resources together in ways many have never considered. Julie has given couples confidence by sharing tangible examples and immediate opportunities to raise support, which can make the incredible journey of adoption more attainable for families. We're thrilled that *You Can Adopt Without Debt: Creative Ways to Cover the Cost of Adoption* will be on shelves."
—Krisha Yanko, Lifeline Children's Services

"The Adopt Without Debt Workshop provides not only practical tools to families who are being crushed under the weight of the cost of adoption but also hope that cost need not be the reason a family says no to adoption. It has helped the families in our adoption ministry more than any other tool we have given them—and they have asked for Julie again this year! Through her workshop and book, Julie has and will continue to be the path by which many children find families!"
—Staci Brown, The Church of Eleven22

"What a great experience we had partnering with Julie for her Adopt Without Debt workshop. The time flew by thanks to Julie's amazing wit and wisdom on a subject that might intimidate others. We'll definitely be back for more in the future."
—D. J. Smith, Just Love Coffee

"Great presentation! So encouraging to hear so many fresh ideas and success stories. Very motivating."—Attendee

"Entertaining and enjoyable."—Attendee

"So much good and encouraging info!"—Attendee

Connect with the Author

I continue to find fantastic fund-raising ideas that adoptive families are using to bring their kids home as well as new adoption grant resources. All this, and tips on living financially free can be found on my blog at juliegumm.com. I hope you'll stop by and say hi. If you come up with a new fund-raiser idea not in the book, I hope you'll come share it with me so as a community we can help one another.
E-mail: julie@juliegumm.com
Twitter: @JulieGumm
Facebook: facebook.com/authorjuliegumm

NOTES

1. The Adoption Adventure

1. U.S. Dept of Health and Human Services, "Trends in Foster Care & Adoption (FFY2002-FFY2012)," Administration for Children and Families, accessed September 17, 2014, acf.hhs.gov/sites/default/files/cb/trends_foster care_adoption2012.pdf.

2. UNICEF, "Children and AIDS: Fifth Stocktaking Report, 2010" (November 2010), accessed September 19, 2014, unicef.org/publications/files /Children_and_AIDS-Fifth_Stocktaking_Report_2010_EN.pdf.

3. "On Understanding Adoption Statistics," Christian Alliance for Orphans (9 July 2012), christianalliancefororphans.org/wp-content/uploads/Christian -Alliance-for-Orphans-_On-Understanding-Orphan-Statistics_.pdf.

4. Anup Shah, "Poverty Facts and Stats," *Global Issues* (January 7, 2013), accessed October 5, 2013, globalissues.org/article/26/poverty-facts-and-stats.

5. Sten Johansson and Ola Nygren, "The Missing Girls of China: A New Demographic Account," *Population and Development Review* (March 1991): 35–51, jstor.org/stable/1972351.

6. "FY 2012 Annual Report on Intercountry Adoption," Office of Children's Issues (January 2013), travel.state.gov/content/dam/aa/pdfs/fy2012_annual _report.pdf.

7. Eliza Newlin Carney, "Domestic Adoption: Perception and Reality," *Adoptive Families Magazine* (2013), accessed June 23, 2013, adoptivefamilies .com/articles.php?aid=1618.

8. Susan Smith, "Safeguarding the Rights and Well-Being of Birthparents in the Adoption Process," Evan B. Donaldson Adoption Institute (January 2007): 26, accessed September 19, 2014, adoptioninstitute.org/old/publica tions/2006_11_Birthparent_Study_All.pdf.

2. What Type of Adoption Is Right for You?

1. "Meet the Children," AdoptUSKids, accessed September 19, 2014, adopt uskids.org/meet-the-children.

2. "Facts and Statistics," Congressional Coalition on Adoption Institute, accessed September 19, 2014, ccainstitute.org/index.php?option=com_content &view=category&layout=blog&id=25&Itemid=43.

3. "5 Reasons You Won't Adopt from Foster Care, and Why They're Wrong," Dave Thomas Foundation for Adoption (November 29, 2012), accessed June 23 2013, davethomasfoundation.org/5-reasons-you-wont-adopt-from -foster-care-and-why-theyre-wrong/.

4. "The Most Frequently Asked Questions about Adoption," Dave Thomas Foundation for Adoption, accessed June 23, 2013, davethomasfoundation.org /about-foster-care-adoption/faqs/.

5. Kelly Porter, "What a Foster-To-Adoption Process Is Really Like," *The Huffington Post* (January 8, 2013), accessed June 23, 2013, huffingtonpost .com/2013/01/18/foster-to-adoption-process_n_2496567.html.

6. Eliza Newlin Carney, "Domestic Adoption: Perception and Reality," *Adoptive Families Magazine*, accessed September 19, 2014, adoptivefamilies. com/articles.php?aid=1618.

7. "Timing of Adoption Update: 2010–2011," *Adoptive Families Magazine* (2013), accessed June 23, 2013, adoptivefamilies.com/articles.php?aid=2351.

8. "Consent to Adoption by State," ABC Adoptions, accessed June 23, 2013, abcadoptions.com/consent1.htm.

9. Deborah H. Siegel and Susan L. Smith, "Openness in Adoption: From Secrecy and Stigma to Knowledge and Connections," Evan B. Donaldson Adoption Institute (2012): 7, accessed September 19, 2014, adoptioninstitute .org/old/publications/2012_03_OpennessInAdoption.pdf

10. Ibid.

11. Gwen Dewar, "Wired for Fast-track Learning? The Newborn Senses of Taste and Smell," *Parenting Science* (2009), accessed September 19, 2014, parentingscience.com/newborn-senses.html.

12. "FY 2012 Annual Report on Intercountry Adoption," Office of Children's Issues (January 2013), accessed September 19, 2014, travel.state.gov/content /dam/aa/pdfs/fy2012_annual_report.pdf.

13. "Statistics," Intercountry Adoption, U.S. Department of State (2012), accessed September 19, 2014, travel.state.gov/content/dam/aa/pdfs/fy2012 _annual_report.pdf.

3. Choosing an Agency or Attorney

1. Mark T. McDermott, "Independent Adoptions," *Adoptive Families Magazine*, accessed December 29, 2013, adoptivefamilies.com/articles.php ?aid=1017.

2. "Adoption: Guatemala," The Schuster Institute for Investigative Journalism (March 8, 2012), accessed January 20, 2013, brandeis.edu/investi gate/adoption/guatemala.html.

3. Jen Hatmaker, "Examining International Adoption Ethics, Part Two," jenhatmaker.com/blog/2013/05/20/examining-adoption-ethics-part-two, accessed September 24, 2014. Part one of the post is found at jenhatmaker.com /blog/2013/05/14/examining-adoption-ethics-part-one.

4. What to Expect in the Process

1. "Timing of Adoption Update: 2012–2013," *Adoptive Families Magazine*, accessed September 25, 2014, adoptivefamilies.com/articles/1133 /domestic-international-foster-adoption-timelines-2012-2013.

2. "Beyond Culture Camp: Promoting Healthy Identity Formation in Adoption," Evan B. Donaldson Adoption Institute (November 2009): 6, accessed September 19, 2014, adoptioninstitute.org/old/publications/2009_11 _BeyondCultureCamp.pdf.

8. It Starts with Sacrifice

1. "Consumer Expenditures," U.S. Department of Labor (September 10, 2013), accessed September 17, 2014, bls.gov/news.release/cesan.nr0.htm.

2. "Americans Spend $151 a Week on Food; the High-Income, $180," August 2, 2012, accessed September 25, 2014, gallup.com/poll/156416/amer icans-spend-151-week-food-high-income-180.aspx.

3. Phil LeBeau, "Americans Borrowing Record Amount to Buy Cars," CNBC, March 4, 2014, accessed September 25, 2014, cnbc.com/id/101461972#.

10. Employer Benefits

1. "2013 Best Adoption-Friendly Workplaces," Dave Thomas Foundation for Adoption, accessed January 25, 2014, davethomasfoundation.org/news _story/americas-100-best-adoption-friendly-workplaces-recognized-by-the -dave-thomas-foundation-for-adoption/.

2. "Your Benefits—Adoption," National Military Family Association, accessed November 11, 2013, militaryfamily.org/your-benefits/adoption /reimbursement/.

3. "Adoption Benefits Fact Sheet," Dave Thomas Foundation, accessed September 19, 2014, davethomasfoundation.org/about-foster-care-adoption /research/read-the-research/fact-sheet/.

4. See taxalmanac.org/index.php/Internal_Revenue_Code_Sec._137.html.

12. Fund-Raising

1. Curtis Honeycutt, "2 Things to Consider Before Starting Your Next Adoption Fund-Raiser," February 3, 2014, accessed September 25, 2014, juliegumm.com/2014/02/2-reasons-to-think-twice-before-starting-your -next-adoption-fundraiser-guest-post/.

13. Event Fund-Raisers

1. J. T. Olson (founder of Lifesong for Orphans), in discussion with the author, October 2011.

2. Ibid.

17. Adoption Tax Credit

1. A tip from Bills Tax Service, accessed September 23, 2014, centralia -il-taxservice.com/.

18. Giving Back

1. Tom Davis, *Fields of the Fatherless* (Colorado Springs: David C. Cook, 2008), 119.

Made in the USA
Lexington, KY
05 May 2018